AMERICAN HATE

AMERICAN
HATE

SURVIVORS SPEAK OUT

EDITED BY

ARJUN SINGH SETHI

THE
NEW
PRESS

NEW YORK
LONDON

Requests for permission to reproduce selections from this book should be mailed to:
Permissions Department, The New Press, 120 Wall Street, 31st floor, New York, NY
10005.

Published in the United States by The New Press, New York, 2018
Distributed by Two Rivers Distribution

ISBN 978-1-62097-372-1 (e-book)

LIBRARY OF CONGRESS CATALOGING-IN-PUBLICATION DATA
Names: Sethi, Arjun Singh, editor.
Title: American hate : survivors speak out / edited by Arjun Singh Sethi.
Description: New York : New Press, [2018] | Includes bibliographical
    references.
Identifiers: LCCN 2018017581 | ISBN 9781620973714 (hc : alk. paper)
Subjects: LCSH: Victims of hate crime—United States. | Hate crimes—United
    States. | Racism—United States—History—21st century. | United
    States—Race relations—History—21st century. | United States—Politics
    and government—2017-
Classification: LCC HV6773.52 .A44 2018 | DDC 362.88—dc23 LC record
available at https://lccn.loc.gov/2018017581

The New Press publishes books that promote and enrich public discussion and
understanding of the issues vital to our democracy and to a more equitable world.
These books are made possible by the enthusiasm of our readers; the support of a
committed group of donors, large and small; the collaboration of our many partners
in the independent media and the not-for-profit sector; booksellers, who often hand-
sell New Press books; librarians; and above all by our authors.

www.thenewpress.com

Book design and composition by Bookbright Media
This book was set in Sabon and Nosta

Printed in the United States of America

10 9 8 7 6 5 4 3

To the silenced and unheard,
to my mother, who is strong and compassionate,
in gratitude and promise

CONTENTS

AMERICAN HATE

INTRODUCTION

AMERICAN HATE

THIS IS A BOOK ABOUT PEOPLE WHOSE LIVES HAVE BEEN impacted by hate. It is a book about communities under threat. It is a book about pain, struggle, and resilience.

Hate comes in many forms: vicious intimidation and cyber-trolling; vandalism and arson of houses of worship; and assault or even murder on your own doorstep. It also comes in the form of government regulations and policies: banishing immigrants and separating them from their families because they do not have papers; depriving the elderly, poor, communities of color, and people with disabilities of health care; appropriating Native lands and resources; and threatening to send refugees home where they would face an uncertain future. People are targeted across this country because of their race, national origin, sex, gender identity, sexual orientation, faith, disability, immigration status, and other personal characteristics.

We must begin by acknowledging that this country was built

on a hate crime. The Native people of this land were displaced and exterminated to make room for Christians and Europeans. Hate has been a fixture of our country for as long as it has existed. Land theft, slavery, segregation, xenophobia, and exclusion are defining features of our history. So is the ideology of white supremacy, the belief that the white race is superior to all others. It is why we segregated black people from white people after slavery and allowed Jim Crow laws to flourish; allowed mobs and vigilantes to roam freely and lynch black people at will; banned the Chinese from immigrating in 1882; and incarcerated more than 100,000 Japanese Americans during World War II.

We have also seen that hate violence can strike at any time and is often used to keep vulnerable communities in their place. In 1907, a rabble of five hundred white men assaulted more than one hundred South Asian workers in Bellingham, Washington, locked them in the basement of city hall, and then forced them out of town.[1] In 1963, known Ku Klux Klansmen bombed the 16th Street Baptist Church in Birmingham, Alabama, killing four girls and injuring others. In 1998, two men tortured and murdered Matthew Shepard in Laramie, Wyoming, because he was gay. And in 2015, an avowed white supremacist, Dylann Roof, murdered nine people at the Emanuel African Methodist Episcopal Church in Charleston, South Carolina. Hate and discrimination are not new; they are part of our country's DNA. Throughout it all, targeted communities have learned a painful lesson. The promises of equality under the law and freedom from harm are often the most enduring and dangerous illusions of American life.

In this book, you will find stories about hate and its terrible consequences in America. And while it is a fact that communities of color, immigrants, people of faith, and others have long faced hate in this nation, something has changed during these past few years. I have spoken and met with organizers, activists, and policy advocates; and sat down with survivors of hate in their offices, universities, community centers, houses of worship, and homes. They all say something similar. The 2016 presidential campaign and subsequent election of Donald J. Trump emboldened, empowered, enabled, facilitated, and legitimized the very worst in America: racism, xenophobia, Islamophobia, sexism, anti-Semitism, homophobia, transphobia, ableism, and anti-immigrant hostility. Much of what we see today is an outgrowth of what we have experienced before, but the hate nowadays is more visceral and widespread than many of us could have imagined just a few years ago.

There are many who ask why President Trump does not condemn acts of hate and bigotry, and when he does, why it takes him so long. But Trump told us who he was a long time ago, and it is time we believed him. He is a racist and a sexist, and his ideologies are white supremacy and greed. He is the hater-in-chief, and his history, rhetoric, and policies show it.

Trump was twice accused of discriminating against African American renters in New York City. He bought full-page newspaper ads calling for the execution of the Central Park Five, five young men of color who were arrested for attacking a jogger, and he continued to proclaim their guilt even after they were exonerated. As a casino owner, he ordered black employees off his casino floors during his visits and called them "lazy." He secretly funded anti-Native ads featuring pictures of cocaine and syringes, and insulted a group of Natives during a Congressional hearing, saying, "They don't look like Indians to me." He was a leading proponent of birtherism, a movement to delegitimize former president Barack Obama.[2] He has also demeaned women and treated them abusively throughout his public life and even bragged about committing sexual assaults on camera.[3]

Trump's presidential campaign was an extension of this ugly and virulent worldview. He called Mexican undocumented immigrants "rapists"; ridiculed Chinese and Japanese trade negotiators using broken English; defended two white men who assaulted a Latino man as "passionate" supporters; criticized a judge because he was Mexican; approved the beating of a

Black Lives Matter protester; mocked a reporter with a disability; stereotyped Jews as cunning negotiators; declared that "Islam hates us"; and repeatedly called an elected official of Native heritage "Pocahontas."[4]

Trump stirred racial divides and fanned white anxiety throughout his campaign. White nationalist, neo-Nazi, racist skinhead, and anti-Muslim groups were already on the rise, and Trump courted them with his speeches, retweets, and deafening silence. Some of these organizations are new and were created after the election of President Obama, while others, like the Ku Klux Klan, date back more than one hundred years. They vary in size, structure, and resources, but their members share a common belief that they are superior to others. Trump spoke of a disappearing history and culture, and nativists felt vindicated. Their white privilege was renewed, and they celebrated "Make America Great Again" with thunderous applause. Trump said he wanted to restore the waning demographic and economic power of the hinterland, and when he blamed immigration and trade, rather than corporate excess and technological disruption, many believed him and ignored his racism. He openly ridiculed and insulted women, and some men felt restored. He rarely mentioned the words white, straight, Christian, or men, but it was clear to whom he was appealing.

As president, he has sought to build a border wall, ban Muslims and refugees, deport the Dreamers, rescinded protections for transgender students, rolled back efforts to reform police departments, and blocked future civil rights investigations.[5] In discussions in the Oval Office relating to immigration, he reportedly claimed that Haitians "all have AIDS," Nigerians would never "go back to their huts," and Haiti and African nations were "shithole countries."[6] He has refused to condemn white supremacists who supported him and has appointed race baiters with a history of prejudice to key cabinet and adviser posts. For instance, Attorney General Jeff Sessions had been denied a federal judgeship in 1986 because of his racist beliefs.[7]

CIA Director Mike Pompeo has close ties to anti-Muslim groups and has accused Muslim American leaders of being "potentially complicit" in terrorism.[8] Former adviser Sebastian Gorka had been fired by the FBI for his Islamophobic rhetoric and later appeared on national television wearing a medal associated with Nazi sympathizers.[9] Trump's aide Stephen Miller planned farcical "Islamofascism Awareness Week" events as a college student and was the chief architect of the first Muslim and refugee travel ban.[10] The now disgraced Steve Bannon, his former chief strategist, has known ties to white nationalists and has identified himself as a nationalist.[11]

This is just a sampling of Trump's hate and bigotry. It may seem redundant and exhaustive to detail this history here, but the painful reality is that many Americans still equivocate or justify Trump's rhetoric and policies towards disenfranchised communities. *He is misunderstood,* some say. *He is playing politics. He has diverse friends.* These beliefs ignore the pain of the communities he maligns; embolden those who share his views; and deny the ideology underlying so much of his hate. His words and actions have real consequences and will be more than a footnote in world history.

There is also something very different and pernicious about a candidate seeking the highest office in the land using his rank, privilege, and power to target others. Now that he is president, he is exercising the worst form of bully pulpit. Trump has fostered hate on the basis of almost every human characteristic including race, faith, disability, sex, gender identity, sexual orientation, weight, national origin, age, immigration status, and class. If you are a white straight cisgender man, a Christian citizen, and do not have a disability, you are likely safe. Otherwise you are a target in Trump's America.

His victory has laid bare the fragility of the progress we thought we had achieved. We have seen that many Americans share his hateful ideology or, at a minimum, are comfortable bystanders to it. The projects of diversity and inclusion, and racial equity and justice, have been badly bruised and many of our hard-earned civil rights victories and social advances have proven to be illusory or, at the very least, capable of being quickly undone through repeal, repeal and replace, and virulent nativism.

The culmination is an open season on marginalized and diverse communities across this country. Hate now braids through our daily lives. We encounter it in the classroom, office, neighborhood, and public life. Sometimes we experience incidents of bias that do not amount to criminal behavior, while at other times we experience the most heinous of crimes. A recent poll of educators found that 25 percent of respondents, or roughly 2,500 people, reported fights, threats, assaults, and other incidents in schools that could be traced to the election.[12] Another study found that more than one in six girls ranging between the ages of fourteen and eighteen have been harassed since Trump's election.[13] Universities and campus groups have been targeted in hundreds of documented incidents spanning more than one hundred universities.[14] Cemeteries, houses of worship, and other sacred sites have been vandalized, including sixty-three mosques between January and July 2017.[15] Entire towns and cities have come under assault by white supremacist, neo-Nazi, and anti-Muslim marches, with Charlottesville being just one example. In the "Unite the Right" rally in August 2017, a coalition of hate mongers, many armed with tiki torches, defended Confederate statues, repudiated America's diversity, and called for a return to the days of old.[16]

Many have paid the ultimate price. Khalid Jabara was murdered in Tulsa, Oklahoma, in August 2016 by his next-door neighbor, a man who had previously insulted and terrorized his family.[17] Srinivas Kuchibhotla was murdered in Kansas City in February 2017 by a man who yelled, "Get out of my country," before shooting him.[18] James Jackson was murdered in New York City in March 2017 by a man whose sole intention was to hurt black people.[19] Richard W. Collins III, a black student, was murdered on the campus of the University of Maryland in May

2017 by a college student associated with a white supremacist group.[20] Just a few days later, Ricky Best and Taliesin Myrddin Namkai-Meche were stabbed to death by a known white supremacist in Portland, Oregon, after they stood up for two girls on a public train.[21] Nabra Hassanen was murdered in June after she left her mosque in Sterling, Virginia, in what her father believes was a hate crime even though police contended otherwise.[22] Heather Heyer was mowed down in Charlottesville after she took to the streets in a counterprotest to the "Unite the Right" rally. At least twenty-seven transgender people, many of them black transgender women, were killed in 2017 because of hate or in otherwise suspicious circumstances.[23] These are just examples. Hate in its various forms makes the news every day in Donald Trump's America.

We also experience hate at the hands of the state through aggressive overreach and deprivation. When the president of the United States calls Mexicans "rapists" and "criminals" and compares Syrian refugees to "snakes," it is hard not to see the wall, the mass deportations, and the banning of refugees as direct attacks on our own lives and families.[24] When the government rescinds rules that would protect transgender students in bathrooms and rolls back police reforms that would protect communities of color, they put a target on our backs.[25] There is also police violence, which acutely impacts black and Native persons, and has continued unabated. Not even viral videos can stop it. The government profiles our communities on the basis of who we are and what we believe.

This is one of my own points of entry. I am particularly sensitive to the rising tide of hate violence and profiling because of my Sikh American identity. Sikhs are targeted because of their articles of faith, and we experience a high incidence of police and government profiling, especially at airports and on planes. I was bullied as a kid and harassed and attacked as an adult, and have been arbitrarily stopped and questioned by police. In researching this book, I was nearly driven off the road in Tulsa, Oklahoma; stared down by a cashier and a customer in a grocery store in Kalispell, Montana; and intentionally misdirected on the campus of American University in Washington, DC.

There have never been reliable statistics documenting hate in America. The FBI collects data on hate crimes, but their figures are grossly incomplete. They rely on local law enforcement agencies to report hate crimes, but reporting remains voluntary, not mandatory. Many localities do not report, and there is no punishment for failing to do so. In 2016, for example, the FBI documented 6,121 hate crimes, but the National Crime Victimization Survey suggests that there could be as many as 250,000 hate crimes a year.[26]

Many hate crimes go unreported because people fear retaliation, shaming, a lackluster government response, government surveillance, deportation if they are undocumented, or revealing their sexual orientation. There are also those who recoil in hateful times or change their identity because of it. Although these people often recede into the shadows, their stories must be shared and heard. In addition, many painful forms of hate are protected under the First Amendment, and yet still others are sponsored by the state. An armed protest outside a mosque by people yelling terrible slurs about Islam and the arrest of an undocumented child after she leaves a hospital are extraordinarily hateful acts, but they are not deemed to be crimes under current laws.

Still, activists across the country have observed a spike in hate incidents in their communities.[27] As an activist and civil rights lawyer who has worked closely with Muslim, Arab, South Asian, and Sikh communities for years, including helping survivors move past hate and representing victims of profiling in court, I too have noticed an uptick. The statistics bear this out. The Southern Poverty Law Center documented more than 1,094 incidents of bias and hate in just the first thirty-four days following the November election.[28] And the latest year for which the FBI has released hate crime data, 2016, shows a sharp rise in hate crimes over the preceding year, including a 20 percent rise in anti-Muslim hate crimes, and a steady increase throughout the year.[29]

Some of these stories and crimes are profiled in this book. The relevant period for these narratives spans the heart of the presidential campaign and the subsequent inauguration of Donald Trump. The first incident profiled occurred in December 2015, six months after Trump announced his candidacy, and the latest incident occurred in May 2017, several months after his inauguration. The pages that follow are not for the faint of heart, but neither is this moment. The rhetoric and policies of this administration, and the hate and bigotry of everyday people, have terrorized communities in ways that we still cannot fully comprehend.

In this book, you will find stories of bullying, trolling, exclusion, banishment, deprivation, stigma, police brutality, appropriation, discrimination, vandalism, arson, assault, and murder. Asmaa Albukaie is a Syrian refugee living in Boise, Idaho, who fears banishment and hate violence. Taylor Dumpson was elected student body president at American University, only to find nooses hanging across campus on her first day in office. Haifa, Victoria, and Rami Jabara lost their beloved family member, Khalid Jabara, to a violent hate crime in Tulsa, Oklahoma. Jeanette Vizguerra is an undocumented mother of four who took sanctuary in a church in Denver, Colorado, after authorities ordered her removal. Alexandra Brodsky was viciously harassed and trolled online because of her faith and her identity as a gender violence survivor. Sarath Suong is the executive director of the Providence Youth Student Movement in Rhode Island, an advocacy organization whose offices were vandalized. Marwan Kreidie is the spokesperson for the Al-Aqsa Islamic Society in Philadelphia, Pennsylvania, at whose mosque a severed pig's head was found outside the front door. Shahid Hashmi is the spokesperson for the Victoria Islamic Center in Texas, a mosque that was burned to the ground.

Tanya Gersh and her family were stalked, trolled, and intimidated by known white nationalists and neo-Nazis who later
threatened to march on her home in Whitefish, Montana. Harjit
Kaur planned an emergency intervention after learning that her
young Sikh American nephew was being bullied in California.
Walia Mohamed and Destinee Mangum were passengers on a
public train in Portland, Oregon, when two men lost their lives,
and a third was badly injured, trying to protect them. Dominick
Evans rarely publicly identifies as a trans man because he fears
for his safety. The lives of Khalid Abu Dawas and other students at New York University were threatened because of their
pro-Palestinian activism. And Ruth Hopkins endured brutal
and excessive force at the hands of law enforcement at Standing
Rock, her birthplace.

The suffering and pain in these stories is sometimes hard to
bear, and I experienced many moments of outrage and sadness
in gathering them and editing this book. But alongside the grief,
you will find stories of survival and resistance. You will even find
unexpected and stirring examples of reconciliation and forgiveness in the most trying and painful of circumstances. A single
hateful act can reveal the worst in humanity, and the response
the most compassionate.

Documenting and sharing these stories right now is particularly important because we live in a damaged reality. Fake news,
or at least the accusation of it, is real. Survivors of hate are dis-
credited, accused of seeking attention, and even charged with
embellishment and fabrication. Many do not come forward
because they fear they will be shamed. These stories will hopefully dispel some of the mythology about hate in America, and
allow impacted communities to unequivocally reclaim the truth.
Hate is real.

There is no better way to tell these stories than in the words
of survivors. For too long, the stories of those who have lost
so much have been told by others. When the media produces
content about vulnerable communities, they tend to marginalize

and exclude us. Our experiences are described and depicted by people we do not know, and our pain and hurt are reduced to a single headline or sound bite. In the Trump era in particular, it has become almost trendy to speak, write, produce, and direct material about marginalized communities. But rarely do the purveyors of content sit down and speak at length with survivors. Rarely do they visit them in their homes. Rarely do they see how hate has impacted their everyday lives, their communities, and those around them. The survivors in this book repeatedly expressed this concern.

The testimonial format allows each survivor to tell their own story in their own words. I spoke with each survivor at length, most often in person, transcribed their interview, and then edited it for length, clarity, and structure. In some cases, they supplemented these drafts with additional content. There is a real and growing concern among activists that we increasingly traffic stories. When survivors come forward and are given a meaningful platform, they are often whisked away to a city they do not know, to sit down with audiences they have never met. It can quickly become exploitative because the trauma that survivors endure is deep, personal, and hard to share. I did everything in my power to avoid this. The survivors were involved and consulted at every stage in the process, and had the final say on what was included. Their comfort, emotional well-being, and mental health always came first. In addition, after the book is published, I hope to convene community conversations with the survivors across the country on how to combat hate.

In these testimonials, you will learn about people's identities, values, and struggles; the history of their communities and the challenges they endure; how the hate incidents affected the survivors and their communities; and how they moved forward and, in some cases, thrived and endured despite it all. They are a window into what so many of us see and hear, but do not understand or choose to ignore.

Testimonials also get us closer to a real set of solutions.

Impacted persons and marginalized communities play little to no role in the formulation of the policies, programs, rules, and ethics that govern their lives. If we want to know how to curb, identify, and respond to hate, we should ask them. If we want to know how to document, heal, and move past hate, we should seek their counsel. We must center vulnerable communities in our policy and advocacy discussions because they have lived it. As you will see in the pages of this book, they have so many of the answers we desperately seek, if only we would take the time to listen.

A book like this can never be complete. Hate is a part of daily life in America, and much of it goes unreported, silenced, and unheard. There are additional stories that I wanted to include, but in some cases the survivors were not ready to share their stories because of their trauma; had shared their stories previously and did not want to endure the trauma of sharing it again; or they did not know me personally. In the process of documenting narratives, trust and comfort are critical.

You will find Native, black, Arab, Latinx, South Asian, Southeast Asian, Muslim, Jewish, Sikh, undocumented, refugee, transgender, queer, and disabled voices in this book. You will also find numerous individuals who are members of multiple disenfranchised communities. Black Muslims, transgender people with disabilities, and queer brown community members, for example, often experience the most severe and damaging forms of hate. Being at the crossroads of multiple forms of identity and expression makes them easily identifiable and visceral targets. They are also more vulnerable because they do not fit neatly into a single community, and consequently sometimes are not as rooted as others are.

Hate is often described and treated in siloed ways, and sometimes for good reason. We cannot flatten our diverse experiences and singular struggles in America and strip away their uniqueness. But we can learn from one another, understand what we have in common, and build solidarity across our communities. We can combat hate by understanding the history and many manifestations of white supremacy. This single ideology is responsible for some of the greatest tragedies in modern history, and much of what we see and feel today is just its latest incarnation.

This book centers the perspectives of women and young people. It is women of color who are on the front lines—mobilizing, resisting, and protecting our communities from state and public harm. They have always been the first line of defense for our communities, and today is no different. Many continue to fight tirelessly for their own liberation, and for others', only to have their voices ignored, diminished, co-opted, and drowned out by hate, but also by sexism, misogyny, harassment, and assault.

Like women, youth are on the front lines, especially in schools and on college campuses, where a battle for the soul of this country is under way. It is youth who are building the coalitions of tomorrow and challenging the generational biases within their own communities. They are regular targets of hate as well. Change often begins with young people, and the future will be no different. We elected Trump. Now let us see what the imagination of our youth has to offer.

Many of the survivors also come from modest economic circumstance. This too was intentional. Low income individuals and communities are disproportionately subject to hate by everyday people and government authorities.

Reading the stories that follow is an extraordinary honor and privilege. Consider it a gift from survivors. They want to leave the world a better place than they found it. As I have traveled across the country, I have come to realize that in many ways the purpose of hate is to silence. It seeks to subjugate and exterminate, and to do away with difference and uniqueness. The individuals whose stories you will now read refuse to be silenced. Speaking out is the most basic and vital form of resistance.

1

ASMAA ALBUKAIE

In his first week in office, Trump banned nationals from seven Muslim-majority countries and refugees from entering the country. Numerous courts struck down large portions of the ban, prompting the White House to promulgate different versions in subsequent months. In October 2017, Trump ended the ban on refugees, but called for a ninety-day review of the refugee program for nationals from eleven countries considered "high-risk." The refugee admissions program was resumed but with enhanced "extreme vetting." Trump also capped refugee admissions at 45,000 for 2018, the lowest level in decades.

Asmaa Albukaie is a Syrian refugee who lives in Boise, Idaho. She arrived in the United States with her two children in November 2014.

MY TWO CHILDREN AND I ARRIVED IN BOISE JUST AFTER MID-night. I thought everybody would be asleep, and we would have nowhere to go. Then two people in the luggage area saw me and introduced themselves. One was my case manager from the Agency for New Americans, an organization that helps refugees, and the other was a translator. They told me that my apartment wasn't ready, but that I had a room in a nearby hotel.

They took me to my room and explained how to come and go from the hotel and use the electronic key, and pointed out other features of the room. They had an Arabic dinner ready for us so that we would feel welcome. I was happy with the food, but would have been just as pleased with pizza. My kids and I were awake most of the night. We were more excited than tired. We kept looking out the window, waiting for the sun to rise. We wanted to see our new home.

When we awoke, it was snowing. We left the hotel and looked around. I was so excited to see the trees and new faces. People probably thought I was staring at them, but I couldn't hide my relief. I walked to the nearest grocery store, while the kids played in the snow. We were the first Syrian refugee family to be resettled in Idaho.

I had never thought I would leave Damascus. I got married when I was young and raised two young boys in Syria. For the first few years of my marriage, I was a housewife and tended to our children and home. I later got a bachelor's degree in library science, enrolled in a master's program at Damascus University, and taught a class in library science at the university. Education was always important to me.

Everything changed when the war broke out. My husband was taken and killed during the civil war. I think it was a case of mistaken identity because he wasn't very political. He was a doctor and returning from a stay in Turkey. Then my children were kidnapped, and I had to borrow money from my dad to pay the ransom. I learned quickly that terrible things happen in war. Thousands died in Syria, and many more fled. I saw unspeakable terror and atrocity. I try not to think about it very much because it's so painful. My decision to leave was difficult because I was a single mom. I was very close to my family, got married when I was young, and had no idea how to follow my own path. But we had to leave. We feared for our lives. My children, especially, were at risk.

I left Syria for Egypt in May 2013 with my two boys. They were thirteen and fourteen. We packed our entire lives into a few small bags. We didn't fly because we feared the government would stop us. So we took a bus to Jordan, then a train to the Sinai peninsula in Egypt, and finally a bus to Cairo. It was a long journey.

Many in the Middle East call Egypt *Om El Donya*, or "Mother of the World." I thought Egypt would be safe for the children and a great place to build a future, but it wasn't. I felt excluded, and so did the kids. People didn't want to be around refugees, even if we spoke the same language. I also faced discrimination and sexual harassment, being a single mom, and the police wouldn't help. "You are Syrian. We cannot help you. If you don't feel safe, go back to your country."

I was lucky to find a good job. A local church that worked closely with the Syrian refugee community in Cairo wanted case managers who knew English and were familiar with Syrian culture. I loved watching American movies when I was young and put those skills to good use. It was a secure job and paid the rent.

I registered with the UN Refugee Agency [also known by its formal acronym, UNHCR] shortly after I arrived and applied for asylum. Syrians aren't allowed to stay in Egypt as tourists or visitors, and must register as asylum seekers with the UNHCR. "Did you lose family members in Syria?" "Why did you leave?" "Will you hurt others?" I had a series of interviews and answered all of their questions. I also reported the sexual harassment to the UNHCR, hoping they would protect me and punish those who harassed me. It was only later that I learned they aren't a police force, they just resettle refugees.

They asked me if I was interested in leaving Egypt and relocating elsewhere. I said yes and asked where I would be sent, but they never told me. I then had numerous additional interviews with government officials, whose titles and affiliations were never clear to me. Those were long days. I would travel to the site in the morning and wait hours for my turn. The interview rooms were small and had no windows. They would inspect my documents and ask me the same questions every time. The officials never reacted and wouldn't tell me when a decision on my case would be made. It was difficult to share my story so many times with so many different people. I was in so much pain.

Then one day I received a phone call saying the U.S. had accepted me as a refugee. Refugees can't choose where they will be resettled, but the U.S. would have been my first choice. I wanted to work hard, earn my own money, and build a life as a single mom. That was my dream.

Weeks later, and just days before I left, I received my transportation paperwork. It read "Boise, ID." I didn't know "Boise" or "ID." So I googled it and saw beautiful images of the mountains and downtown. I thought I would grow to love this place because I didn't want to be in a crowded city like New York or Washington, DC. But when I called two of my friends, one in the U.K. and the other in the U.S., they said the same thing: potatoes and snow. They said there was nothing else in Idaho. I knew they were teasing me, but I took it very seriously. I told the kids that we might have to eat french fries every day and work in the snow. I read everything I could about potatoes and snow because I wanted to be positive, but I was really scared.

The conversations with my children were hard. We didn't know what life would be like in the U.S. The kids were afraid because they didn't speak English. They couldn't even tell the time in English. But they eventually got excited. They had dreams, too.

In November 2014, almost seventeen months after arriving in Egypt, we left for the U.S. We held hands as the plane took off, and cried and laughed. We were excited about leaving Egypt and scared about our uncertain future. There were four flights in total: Egypt to Germany, to Chicago, to Utah, to Idaho. Every time the plane landed, we looked at each other in relief.

Our first few months in Boise were very hard. We had complete culture shock and missed our family. I didn't know how to pay the bills or drive a car. The financial support we received was just enough to survive. I got sick and thought I would lose my Medicaid just because I was a refugee. I had trouble finding a job because I didn't have the required skills. The kids felt terrible because they couldn't speak English. My younger son would come home from school and cry for hours. "I don't speak English. I want to speak English now. I want to make friends." One of his teachers called me, crying, because she was so sad for him.

I eventually found a job as an interpreter for a local mental health clinic. Some of the clients were Arab, and they needed female interpreters. Then I found an apartment. Finally, some months later, I was hired by the Agency for New Americans, the same agency that supported me, to be a resettlement officer. It was wonderful. I was helping refugees just like me.

Part of the culture shock was the reaction of some of the people in Boise. I was at the grocery store in my first week there and mistakenly tapped a man with my grocery cart. "You're crazy because of that thing on your head," he said, referring to my hijab. I froze, then smiled at him and said, "Sorry, I didn't see you. I'm new to this country and I look at everything, even in the grocery store." He walked off. I felt very sad afterwards. Then, some weeks later, I was going into the bank as another woman was leaving. She saw my scarf and said, "Oh my God, the Muslims are coming." I wanted to introduce myself and share my story, but the woman looked terrified.

I had many other incidents like this. When I was learning to drive and would make small mistakes on the road, people would yell things like "Fucking Muslim" or "ISIS." I would always smile back and say, "I'm not crazy. I'm a new driver and I have just come to this country." Another time a lady said, "I like your personality, but I don't like Muslim women with scarves. I'm afraid they're hiding a bomb in their hair."

Then in February 2016, my son came home one evening with a terrible bruise on his face. He told me what had happened: "I was with my friend, and a big American guy came up to me and asked, 'Are you Muslim?' I said, 'Yes, I am Muslim.' Then he punched me in the face. I cried. Then my friend called the police. The police officer was very nice to me and prepared a report."

He was very clear. Still, I thought he must have done something wrong. As refugees, we're always afraid that the police or the government will send us home, even when we're the victims. All was made clear the next day when I received a call saying that my son was in fact the victim of a hate crime.

I don't want to say much about the incident because my son is still young. But everything changed for him that day. He became less trusting, and it was harder for him to make new friends. His language skills suffered, too. One day he asked me, "Should I lie next time? If people ask me if I'm Muslim, should I tell them I'm not?" I told him he should be proud to be a good Muslim and proud of his identity. I hope he listens.

I went to the last hearing in the court case because the judge asked me for a statement. I told the judge that the man in the courtroom who hurt my son wouldn't learn love and respect from a jail cell. He needed to be educated. He needed to learn that we're refugees who ran away from war, that we seek safety and don't want to hurt anyone, and that Islam is a peaceful religion. I told the judge that I had forgiven the offender and that my forgiveness was an example of how to respect and love others. The judge sentenced him to time in jail and community service.

You have to remember that America gave me so much. It gave my family a second chance. I love and respect the American people, even if some of them hate me. It doesn't matter what people say or do to me. I always smile and try to educate them.

Plus, there were so many people in Boise who did care about us. Throughout my time here, many people have supported my family and welcomed us into this community. I often hear, "Welcome to Idaho. I hope you'll like it here. We're happy for you, and I hope you feel at home here." I have lots of friends in the Jewish and Christian communities.

Still, I'm afraid that we could be targeted again. This country is changing. Donald Trump's campaign was traumatic for me: "We don't know who they are. If I win, the Syrian refugees are going back. I will stop all refugees from coming. We will close our borders." That was scary because our future is in America. I can't imagine leaving and rebuilding our lives elsewhere. Plus, if we were sent back to Syria, we would be killed because the government would know we had fled as asylum seekers. When he later became president and tried to ban Muslims and refugees, I worried that we would be removed. But the lawyers told me that we were protected.

What he says about Muslims is bad. He's encouraged hatred of Muslims, Syrians, and refugees. He tried to ban them and only mentions Muslims as terrorists. We are not human beings to him. I remember on the campaign trail when he kicked out Rose Hamid, a Muslim woman, from one of his rallies for wearing a T-shirt that read "Salaam, I Come in Peace." The crowd treated her so badly.

His comments about refugees are also unfair because it was the U.S. that selected me. While I'm grateful to be here, I didn't choose to be here. They didn't give me money, housing, or a car. Any limited support I received I paid back in taxes. They resettled me for my safety. But where's my safety now?

He's also wrong when he says we don't have documents. We have our passports, birth certificates, and medical papers. My passport is valid until 2019. I presented my documents more than ten times before I was accepted as a refugee in the U.S. His comments are humiliating and dangerous. People will be more scared of us if they don't know we were invited into this country.

When I arrived in the U.S. in November 2014, we experienced hate, but not like today or during the campaign. I'm always careful the day after Trump says something about our communities. I watch people's faces to see if they're scared or are looking at me with hate. People don't always know that I'm from Syria or a refugee, but my head scarf is a daily reminder that I'm a Muslim.

What makes America great is helping people who need it, and giving safety to those searching for it. This country gave my family a home and safety. For me, the U.S. was already great. In 2016, the U.S. resettled more refugees than any other country in the world. But not anymore because Trump is really limiting the number of refugees. This is not the U.S. I know.

Sometimes people ask me if I would ever remove my head scarf now that I'm in America, or because I'm scared. I will never remove it. It's my identity. I love my hijab. It's beautiful. It hugs my face and gives me comfort every day. Freedom for me is being able to express my faith.

I'm proud to work as a resettlement officer and help refugees who are still able to come to this country. The agency helped me stand on my feet, and now I can help others facing the same struggle. I always tell my clients that they can be who they are, love their culture, and still live happily in this country. They don't have to change for anyone. That's what America is about.

When I think back to when I first arrived, I sometimes cry. I remember those first few moments when I was lost in the airport. I remember standing there and not knowing my future. Today, I own a home. I bought it recently and decorated it in a Syrian-American style. I love inviting my American friends over to watch movies and celebrate life.

Trump can be hateful, but I will continue to be welcoming and friendly. I believe everyone has goodness in their heart. Sometimes you just need to break a barrier and jump into their heart. Even if people don't accept us right away, I believe they will with time. That's why I don't turn away or give up when people say hateful or aggressive things. I always smile and share my story, even if I am mad or upset. I give them a chance to learn and talk with me. And I've found that when you give them a chance, they sometimes listen or even say they are sorry.

A lot of Americans have never traveled outside the U.S. They've never visited a Muslim country, had a Muslim friend, or met a refugee. Americans need to know and hear our stories, and put themselves in our shoes. Their ancestors probably came here for a better life, too. How would they feel if they were targeted because of their race or faith?

Muslims, Syrians, and refugees must continue to reach out to others who are different from them and be open. It's difficult because the media and politicians portray us so poorly. People don't understand that we experience trauma and culture shock, and are victims of terrorism, too. But we love America just like anyone else.

2

TAYLOR DUMPSON

Taylor Dumpson is an activist and a recent graduate of American University in Washington, DC.

I WAS THIRTEEN YEARS OLD THE FIRST TIME I HEARD SOMEONE say the word "nigger." I was in seventh grade, and all of my classmates had gathered for a school assembly. Hundreds of us sat on bleachers, and a black student inadvertently poked a white student with his knee. She turned around angrily and called him a "nigger." Later, in class, she asked me if I was mad, and I said yes and told her that she shouldn't have used that word. She started crying, so the white students consoled her and told the teacher. The teacher then told me to get a dictionary, look up the word "nigger," and read the definition out loud. The first definition was a lazy person. As I read it, the teacher interjected and said perhaps that was what the student meant. My teacher ignored the discriminatory and derogatory meaning of the word "nigger" and humiliated me in front of the entire class.

This was just after the first inauguration of President Obama. I was thirteen years old and one of the only black students in my class.

I was raised in Salisbury on the Eastern Shore of Maryland, the home of Harriet Tubman and Frederick Douglass. Seven generations of my family were raised on the Shore, going back to the 1800s. Both of my parents were educators and instilled in me the value of education and its limits. From kindergarten through eighth grade, I was often the only black girl in my class. My parents saw to it that I learned history that wasn't taught in the classroom. My parents would teach me about black history, and my dad would sit down with me often during Black History Month and ask me to write book reports about civil rights leaders and black pioneers. Maya Angelou was one of my favorites.

I wanted to be an astronaut, so my parents told me about Bessie Coleman and Mae Jemison. Bessie was the first African American woman to become a pilot, and Mae the first to fly in space. My parents encouraged me to soar and strive to do my best at everything that I did. They raised me to pioneer, break barriers, and smash ceilings. They told me that I would have to work ten times harder than others because I was a black girl in America. They wanted me to anticipate the challenges I would face and rise above them.

I first experienced racism in elementary school, when the parents of some of my friends wouldn't let me sleep over. I was young and didn't realize what was happening. As I got older, though, I discussed incidents like this with my parents, and realized that I experienced racism in many ways. I remember praising Obama after he was elected president, and a student saying that I only liked Obama because he was black. Students sometimes gave me ugly looks or said derogatory things to me on the lacrosse field if I outran or outmaneuvered them. When I was fifteen years old and visiting family friends, a group of men in a big SUV yelled "Niggers" at my entire family. My dad didn't want us to see him scared, but deep down I knew he was hurting. My mom was in tears, and so was I. My brother was just ten years old at the time.

The murder of Trayvon Martin changed my life. I cried at the dinner table for weeks, telling my parents that it could have been my friends, my sixth-grade brother, or me. I literally felt sick. I began to question and distrust the police, and felt very different about the U.S. My parents and I started having more conversations about anti-black racism in America. We face discrimination in every walk of life, they told me, including access to housing, employment, education, and health care. Our community is disproportionately subject to police stops, police violence, hate violence, and incarceration. I think the murder of Trayvon and the ensuing trial was a generational moment, just like the murder of Emmett Till and *Brown v. Board of Education*. It showed me that our laws and institutions don't always protect people like me.

That was the moment when I put outer space to the side, and decided that I wanted to be an activist and agent for change. Coming from a long line of activists, I was raised to believe in the value of using your voice and serving your community. Both of my parents were members of the NAACP and African American fraternities and sororities. I remember completing my first community service project when I was four years old. So, I got more involved in activism in high school. By then, I had transferred into the minority-majority high school in my town and finally found myself around people who looked like me and thought like me. I finally had a black community other than my family to share my resistance and pain. I later decided that I wanted to study law and society at American University. The school was politically active and had a reputation for social justice.

What I experienced at AU was very different. Michael Brown was murdered during my freshman year, and I thought students would be sympathetic to the Ferguson uprising. Instead, many students justified his murder by citing his past behavior or his alleged failure to follow police instructions. They said he deserved to die. Students would express their views in lots of ways, including through Yik Yak, an online, anonymous messaging app, which was widely used across campus. Yik Yak is defunct now, but at its peak it was one of the ten most downloaded apps on the Web. It was extremely popular on college campuses, and allowed users within a certain radius to share their thoughts anonymously, almost like Twitter. The racism and hate were terrifying. After Ferguson, I remember people saying on Yik Yak:

If you bring the ropes, I'll bring the fire.

There's a bunch of monkeys out on the quad protesting.

Don't protest by the library, some of us are trying to study. Go back to where you came from.

These messages got lots of likes and shares, and appeared every time a black person was killed by the police or their story was in the news. Trayvon Martin, Mike Brown, Sandra Bland, Philando Castile, Eric Garner, and others were all seemingly responsible for their own deaths, and black students who resisted were likened to monkeys or called other derogatory names. It was such a difficult time to be on campus and away from our families because nobody seemed to care. We received so little understanding from our peers. Often, we received hate.

The anonymity in particular scared us. Anyone on campus could have posted and shared the hateful messages: a roommate, or even a professor. Every time there was a microaggression in the classroom or dorm, we feared violence could be next. Throughout those two years, we asked AU to block Yik Yak on university Wi-Fi. Although several schools did ban it because of bullying and harassment, AU prioritized free speech and refused to block the app.

Things got worse in subsequent years. The following summer, just before my sophomore year, Sandra Bland was murdered. She was found hanging in a jail cell, three days after being arrested during a routine traffic stop. I was twenty years old then, and drove back and forth between DC and the Eastern Shore. Sandra could have been me.

My hands still get clammy sometimes when I see cops on the road. Anonymous hateful and racist messages began to appear again. Then, in my junior year, several black freshman girls were the victims of a hate crime. In their first few weeks on campus, bananas were tossed into their rooms or placed outside their doors.

I still remember three girls asking me a few weeks later if things had been as bad when I was a freshman. I told them they were, but also said that staying at AU allowed me to find my voice and develop my passion for racial justice. After that conversation and the subsequent election of Donald Trump, I decided that I would do everything in my power to help underrepresented students at AU find their place there. I decided to run for student government president. I had already joined numerous organizational boards and clubs on campus, and was ready to take the next step. Student office and politics isn't for everyone, but I thought I could make a difference at AU and in the nation's capital. I would be the first black woman to be student government president at AU in its more than one-hundred-year history, and I would serve just down the street from a president who preached hate.

There were four candidates in total; I was the only black one. My campaign slogan was "A [Different] U" because I wanted to galvanize students who felt marginalized or misrepresented. Our platform consisted of five principles: inclusion, accessibility, accountability, transparency, and support. We asked for a space on campus for students of color and allies to meet, heal, and regroup; a stronger communication line with the administration to discuss our concerns; additional resources for mental health and emotional support; and greater diversity across all levels of the university, including staff and professors.

The entire room erupted when they announced my victory. Seeing the freshmen yell in excitement because they had a president that looked like them meant the world to me. I won by just 129 votes. I was sworn in on April 30, 2017.

The very next morning, on May 1, bananas were found hanging from nooses made of black nylon rope in at least three separate locations on AU's campus. The bananas were marked with the letters "AKA," the abbreviation for the historically black sorority Alpha Kappa Alpha, of which I'm a member. One of the bananas read "Harambe bait," a reference to the gorilla killed at the Cincinnati zoo in 2016. The bananas were spread out across campus; one of them was right next to the freshman dorms. Grainy video footage showed a person in a stocking cap hanging them between 4 and 6 a.m. The FBI and DOJ are investigating it as a hate crime.

The entire black community was targeted that day. So was every vulnerable community on campus, all on my first day in office. It was supposed to be a new beginning. Instead, they tried to knock us back down. I was shocked and angry. My dad told me to keep my head up and reminded me that I had earned the title of student government president. I broke down on the phone while talking with my mom about what happened. They both came to AU later that day to be with me. I always had someone by my side those first few days. I kept a brave face on the outside, but was broken inside.

I decided to put out a statement that first day because so many students were terrified. I said that we would get past this together and that all members of our community should feel safe and welcome; and I reminded them of the words of Frederick Douglass: "If there is no struggle, there is no progress." I also told them that being first was never easy.

The response from the student body was strong. Hundreds of students protested and walked out of a university-planned town hall the next day. It was the first time we'd seen our president discuss race on campus, and we couldn't help but wonder why he had needed to have a terrible hate crime occur before he finally spoke out. Many students symbolically signed paperwork that day to withdraw from the school. Although the university put out a statement condemning the incident, many felt that it wasn't strong enough because there were warning signs all along that the school had refused to acknowledge.

That Thursday we held our own student-sponsored town hall and had an extraordinary turnout. Hundreds of people attended, and there was standing room only. Students, faculty, staff, alumni, and even international members of the sorority joined in solidarity. This was important because the incident impacted all diverse students, and our collective safety was under threat. It was the most stirring and heartfelt conversation on race I had ever been a part of at AU.

In one of my most vulnerable moments, my experience with the hate crime went from bad to worse, when the university co-opted a press conference that we, as a student government, had planned. I remember being pulled into a stairwell and given specific instructions by school administrators. I was told where to stand, how to speak, and what to say. I didn't want to upset the school, and did as they asked. After the press conference, they ushered us into a meeting room with big glass windows, where we met with the president and his cabinet. Reporters took photos through the glass, and it felt like I was a fish in a fish tank. I had to cooperate; otherwise, I would have been portrayed as an angry black girl.

I thought the worst was behind me. For four days straight, I had barely slept or eaten, and was looking forward to a good night's rest. But when I got home, I received an email telling me that I was being cybertrolled by neo-Nazis at the Daily Stormer, a white supremacist website with a very active and hateful readership. I had never even heard of the website, but entire articles on it were written about me. I was called a "nigger agitator" and "negress." Someone photoshopped KFC buckets on my head. I don't know how many images and articles ultimately appeared because I stopped checking. It was my first night alone since the hate crime on campus.

I broke down and panicked. It took four days, but it finally hit me. I closed the blinds, shut and locked the doors, and turned the lights off. I crawled into the back corner of my apartment and cried. My life had changed. I didn't know who these people were or what they wanted. But I feared for my life. They had published photos of me, personal information about me, and my social media profiles. My high school lacrosse statistics were no longer my first search result on Google. Hateful images and articles came up instead. I couldn't be alone, so my mom turned around and stayed with me that night. I filed a police report that evening and increased my social media security.

I had been student government president for exactly four days. I took the next ten days off from school to regroup. In the ensuing weeks, I cried often, had nightmares, and struggled with fear and anxiety. I don't remember much because I tried to block it from my mind. I was later diagnosed with PTSD and am presently being treated for it.

Looking back, I can tell you that every act of love and compassion mattered. Diverse students from so many different communities rallied to condemn hate on campus. I received countless letters, emails, and messages of support from all over the world. I keep many of them in a positive-thoughts jar; they always give me comfort. Sorority sisters of mine who are members of the Congressional Black Caucus hosted their own press conference on Capitol Hill that week, and we attended with our international president and regional director. Having strong black women by my side meant everything to me.

We need that kind of unity and solidarity to resist the hateful rhetoric and policies of the Trump administration. I've protested so many times in Washington, DC, and am always encouraged by the diversity of issues and people represented there. We should be protesting the Muslim ban, mass deportations, revocation of transgender rights, the assault on health care, and all the other ways in which communities are under fire. I'm also proud of the diverse coalition that I represent at AU. I work closely with black, Jewish, Muslim, queer, disabled, and undocumented students. White supremacists aren't coming for one of us. They're coming for all of us.

It's also critical to recognize that racism and hatred of black people didn't begin with Trump. It's as old as this country. Unarmed black people have been murdered by police without justification for centuries. Social media just gave it more visibility. We have to tackle the roots of racism, including white supremacy, and remember that Trump exploited long-standing racist and anti-black sentiment. There is no substitute for this deeper work other than difficult conversations. We need to lean into discomfort, because nothing happens when we're comfortable. We have to engage in difficult conversations in our communities and not be afraid of taboos. The less we talk about race, faith, gender identity, sexuality, and the like, the more we fear and hate. Trump mobilized this fear and hate.

Universities have to do a better job of facilitating dialogue on campus as well. Many students turn a blind eye to microaggressions and hate because they aren't impacted by it. But others don't have that luxury. Hate, profiling, and police violence impact some of us every day. If we can't have difficult conversations on campus, where can we? Universities that shirk this responsibility are abandoning their most vulnerable students. As of writing, the Anti-Defamation League has documented 346 incidents of white-supremacist propaganda appearing on college and university campuses since September 1, 2016. More than 200 schools in 44 states and the District of Columbia have been targeted.[1] I worry that the fliers and nooses will one day become guns and mass shootings.

I also think free speech has its limits. It's one thing to have differences of opinion, but quite another to attack another person's humanity. I repeatedly felt threatened by people's words and messages during my time at AU, but we didn't begin to see real change until the physical threat with the nooses. Should it matter? The Daily Stormer turned my online profile from that of a high-school lacrosse star into outright hate overnight. Why should free speech trump emotional well-being? I think we need to better understand how words alone, even those protected by the First Amendment, impact mental health.

Relatedly, universities must be more attentive to the emotional safety and the mental health needs of students, especially if they choose to prioritize free speech over student safety. This is especially true in the present moment, when online bullying, cybertrolling, and anonymous media platforms are spreading and impacting us in hurtful ways.

The same goes for society at large. We used to read about the victims of police violence in the paper and see their photos. Now we watch their death unfold in real time on our cellphones, computers, television screens, and laptops. Many of us are re-traumatized every time we see these viral videos. We need to better understand and treat this collective trauma. I care very deeply about mental health issues because I have seen firsthand how it impacts people on a daily basis. I want to help bring attention to mental health awareness and be a source of hope to survivors of hate and state violence.

Black women have always been at the forefront of civil rights and solidarity work in this country. I'm proud that Black Lives Matter was founded by black women, and I support their vision. When black people are free, we will all be free. But I think we should push ourselves even further. We must remember those who are at the intersection of various forms of marginalization, including black queer and black disabled women. Only when the most vulnerable among us are free, will we all be free. Only then will we rise.

3

HAIFA, VICTORIA, AND
RAMI JABARA

Haifa, Victoria, and Rami Jabara are Christian Lebanese Americans. Their family home is in Tulsa, Oklahoma.

Haifa: We fled Lebanon in 1983 because we wanted to save our children from the death and destruction of the civil war. We fled in the middle of the night, sold all our possessions, and had only $2,000 to our name because the Lebanese currency had collapsed. We settled in Tulsa because my brother worked here as a physician. We had water, electricity, and basic services in Tulsa. There was a small local Lebanese community that supported us. Plus, the neighbors were friendly. We felt safe. But we had difficulty adjusting to our new life. My husband, Mounah, was a hospital administrator and couldn't find a position. We eventually opened a restaurant. I never dreamed I would work in a restaurant, but we had to survive. There were no authentic Middle Eastern restaurants in Tulsa, and we thought it would be a successful business. We started as a small bakery and deli and grew into a full catering company called Limelite Catering. The recipes are from my village in Lebanon. Thirty years later, we still live in Tulsa. We became comfortable here. The kids adjusted, and so did my husband and I.

Rami: We have a strong Lebanese American community in Tulsa today. Some families settled here almost one hundred years ago. Then you had a second round of immigrants, like my parents, who emigrated in the 1970s, 1980s, or 1990s, mostly emigrating because they were fleeing the civil war. Then there's people like my sister and me. We came here when we were very young. I'm the youngest of the three kids, and was only six months old when we settled in Tulsa.

Victoria: There was pressure to assimilate, growing up. The Arab population in Tulsa was small, and we stood out. We tried to blend in. We didn't want to be different. I remember telling my mom, "I don't want to bring Lebanese food to school for lunch." Khalid had it the hardest. He was darker than my brother and I, plus he had an Arabic name.

Haifa: Khalid means "eternal" in Arabic.

Rami: He definitely had it the hardest. Khalid had a darker complexion than my sister and I. We looked "white."

Victoria: And I go by Vicky. Looking back, there's no question that Khalid felt that pain and prejudice more than we did.

Rami: People sometimes called him a "sand-nigger" or a "camel jockey" in middle school and high school. I never really encountered anything like that.

Victoria: Khalid was sensitive. If Rami, my parents, or I were insulted, we'd brush it off or push back. But Khalid would sometimes internalize it, and so it affected him differently. It also made him feel isolated. He felt different from us because he didn't look like us, but he did look like my dad's side of the family.

Rami: But at the same time, Khalid was the most attractive among us by far. People would sometimes chase him like he was a celebrity or famous singer! I was always jealous during middle and high school because the girls would say, "Wait, is that your brother?" or "What's your brother up to?"

Victoria: Sometimes he'd get free stuff at the store! I'm not kidding. He would go to the register and the store clerk would smile and say, "It's on me." When we'd fly, he'd sometimes get a free upgrade to first class. But because he was shy and isolated, he didn't know that he had that effect on people. He didn't believe it.

Rami: As a kid, I always looked up to Khalid. I wanted to do everything he did. He would beat me up, beat up my friends, and defend me, too, just like any other big brother. He taught me so much; he always thought outside the box. He loved all things technology and electronics. If something broke, he would say: "Don't be afraid to try new things. Be creative. Fix things yourself. If you mess up, try again."

Victoria: For me, it was the opposite. He was my sweet (and at times annoying!) little brother who wanted to hang out with my friends. But he was the smart, funny, and best-looking one. And he had an amazing voice! I miraculously convinced him to play the role of Aladdin in his high-school talent show, and he won.

Rami: He had a charm that none of us had. He could talk to anybody—a homeless person, or the richest guy in the room. But he was still an introvert. I can't believe you got him to play Aladdin.

Victoria: Life in Tulsa was generally okay for us. Even after 9/11, I remember feeling worried that the restaurant would be targeted. But nothing happened. People just appreciated the food.

Haifa: I didn't feel threatened after 9/11. Nobody said anything to us.

Victoria: We moved into this house in 2006. Our next-door neighbor was Stephen Schmauss, an elderly man in his seventies. He would help us fix things around the house. Sometimes he'd bring in the mail. He and Khalid became fast friends because they both loved computers and technology. Sometimes they'd build computers in Stephen's home.

Rami: Everything changed when Vernon Majors moved in with the neighbor. He didn't like our family, especially Khalid and my mom. He was filled with hate.

Haifa: I never say his name.

Victoria: When he first arrived at the house next door in 2011, he was angry that my brother had technology and computer equipment there. Majors threw out all of Khalid's stuff. Hard drives, monitors, wires, and much more. Whatever was left there Khalid soon removed because Majors seemed to be in charge.

Haifa: He broke so many things that day. He threw everything out the door.

Victoria: On another occasion, he came onto our property, took pictures of my mom cooking, and called the health department, asking for our business to be shut down. He claimed that we were preparing food for our business at home, which we were not. It got worse from there. He called us "filthy Arabs." We had an African American friend who mowed the lawn for us, and he called him a "nigger."

Haifa: He would call our other neighbor a "dirty Mexican."

Victoria: We spoke to our friends, and they told us that he had violated the terms of his parole in California and that he wasn't allowed to leave that state. We called the cops, and they took him away. He was sent back to California, and we thought he was out of our life for good.

Rami: Six months later, he was released and came back to our neighborhood. He was much worse. He would call my mom's phone and try to scare her. He said he hated her and wanted to kill her.

Haifa: He used dirty language and kept saying "fuck" on the phone. He would sometimes knock on the windows late at night and harass me.

Victoria: He said things like "dirty Arabs," "Aye-rabs," and "Mooslems." We got a restraining order in March 2015. It was easily granted because of the calls, threats, insults, and taking pictures on our property.

Rami: We decided that if he did anything else, we'd call the police. A few months later, we had an Easter get-together at our home, and he yelled at our guests. The cops arrested him. They charged him with violating the protective order, a misdemeanor. He hired a lawyer and posted bond. When he stopped appearing in court for his hearings, they issued a bench warrant for his arrest.

Victoria: I wish they had arrested him. We called the police and told them he was next door. They can't see beyond the paperwork. On paper, it was just a misdemeanor, so they ignored it.

Haifa: I called, too, but they didn't do anything. I don't understand the system.

Rami: Several weeks later, in September, I was on the phone with my mom talking about my wedding when the phone suddenly cut out. I soon realized the phone hadn't disconnected, and I could hear my mom crying out. Then I heard a lady running over and yelling, "Oh my God, there's a lady! There's a shoe! Somebody call 911!" I didn't know what had happened. I thought my mom was inside the house. Meanwhile, I'm yelling into the phone, asking what happened: "Did she fall? Did she have a heart attack? Did she trip?" The police later arrived and said her injuries were more consistent with being struck by a car, not falling down.

Victoria: When I heard the news, I had an immediate gut feeling that the neighbor was behind it. Khalid had the same premonition, called the cops, and told them to look for Majors.

Rami: They found him several hours later at his house trying to change the license plates. The first thing he said was, "How's Haifa? I thought I hit a bunny." We later learned that earlier that day he had called the police on us for an unknown reason and referred to us as "dirty Arabs." It's in the police record.

Haifa: I had major injuries and head trauma: a broken hand, shoulder, ribs, ankle, nose, and a collapsed lung. I had several operations. My face was so bruised. Even now, I always have pain. My shoulder hurts.

Rami: Some people wouldn't have survived that. She was in the intensive care unit for two weeks and regular care for four weeks.

Victoria: Majors later confessed to running over my mom and described us as the "filthy Lebanese" who "throw gay people off rooftops." This was a reference to videos of ISIS throwing gay people off of buildings. Khalid really panicked. He felt like it was his fault. He wanted to protect my mom. He was only the child living at home at the time.

Rami: Majors's bond was initially set at $200,000, but we immediately contacted the district attorney and told them we feared for our lives.

Haifa: We thought of selling the house. We should have left, but it was difficult because my husband is disabled. Finding a house that can accommodate him was hard. Plus, I had trouble moving after the accident. Khalid was a great son. He helped my husband and I get around. He took us to rehab.

Rami: The judge later revoked bond after a motion by the prosecutor. We felt better. Majors would likely get ten or fifteen years for assault and battery, and we would never see him again. We checked the case docket a lot, and everything appeared to be on track. The trial was set for March 2017. We were doing better. My mom was doing better. Things were on the up-and-up. And then one Friday night in late May, Khalid calls me in a panic and tells me that bond was reinstated and granted at $30,000. Apparently, there was a hearing with a new government attorney who didn't know the case history, and when the defense lawyer made an oral motion to reconsider bond, it was granted by the judge. The government attorney didn't object because he hadn't read the case file and because it's customary to grant bond in cases of assault and battery.

Victoria: This case was different, though, because of the history of hate, the repeated violations of the protective order, and the fact that he lived next door. The district attorney in charge of the case didn't even know that bond had been posted. Later that night, I received a phone call through Vine, a service that keeps victims up-to-date about aggressors subject to protective orders. An auto-recorded voice said that Majors had been released. I freaked out. I thought we had to move immediately. But it was difficult finding a home accessible for disabled persons. We needed one level, no stairs, handlebars, and big doors. And why should we move? This was our home.

Haifa: We started to actively look, but we weren't fast enough.

Rami: We demanded that the district attorney's office file a motion to reconsider bond. They agreed, but we knew it would likely have no effect because Majors was already out of custody. Judges who release criminal defendants on bond will almost never place them back in custody unless the defendants commit a new crime or violate the law. Instead, the judge just doubled the bond from $30,000 to $60,000, which Majors had no problem posting. When bond was posted, I remember the judge telling Majors that he couldn't do anything wrong on the outside. He said, "I'm warning you." The judge also said that perhaps he should order Majors to live elsewhere, a suggestion the district attorney supported, but the judge decided against it.

Victoria: There were no conditions on his bond. No ankle monitor, drug testing, alcohol testing. They sent him back home, next door to the family he terrorized.

Haifa: When he was released, we didn't see him much, in part because we were scared and never went outside. But when he did see me, he'd often scream at me.

Rami: We bought additional door locks and door security bars.

Victoria: Rami wanted cameras. We were all scared. Rami didn't want to come home.

Rami: I didn't want anyone to be there. I didn't feel safe. Nobody could feel safe living next to that man, given what had happened.

Haifa: On Friday, August 12, Khalid called me in a panic and told me not to come home. He said Majors had a gun and that it wasn't safe. He told me to stay away. I called him every ten minutes or so and asked if I could come home. He kept saying no. A few calls later, Khalid told me that Majors had beaten Stephen badly, and that Stephen had fled and told Khalid to call the police. Stephen said that Majors was shooting his gun in the house.

Victoria: We think Stephen tried to get Khalid's attention by throwing something at the window. We don't know for sure because Stephen recently passed away from cancer. When Khalid came outside, Stephen yelled, "Call the police! He has a gun!" Stephen said Majors was shooting at him.

Haifa: Khalid called the police and told them he was really scared.

Victoria: They tried to transfer him to non-emergency, but Khalid uncharacteristically yelled, "This is an emergency!" When the police came, he told them Majors had a gun, that he could hear shooting in the house, and that Stephen had fled. The police then knocked on Majors's door, but he didn't open it. They then told Khalid that Majors wasn't answering, and that they couldn't enter because they didn't have a warrant.

Haifa: A few minutes later, that monster called the police from inside his house. He asked why the police were knocking on his door and told them everything was fine.

Rami: It's like Vernon Majors intended to trick the police to assure them that nothing was wrong.

Haifa: About eight minutes after the police left, I was talking with Khalid on the phone when he was shot and killed. I was talking to my son. I was with my son when he was shot. We were talking, then I heard him screaming for help. I knew something terrible had happened.

Victoria: We don't know why Khalid stepped onto the porch. We just don't know. Mom, what did you hear Majors say?

Haifa: "I told you this was coming." That's what he said.

Rami: That's what he said to Khalid. Mom heard it over the phone. Khalid was shot several times.

Haifa: I was shaking. I didn't know what to do. Khalid was screaming, "Help!" I wanted to leave the line open so I could talk to Khalid, but I had to call 911. When I did, they said a neighbor had called and medics were on the way. My husband was inside the house and called, too. He could see that Khalid was shot. He saw him on the porch crying for help. My husband is still so traumatized about what happened that he doesn't even remember calling 911 that day. He barely remembers anything.

Victoria: A neighbor saw what happened and ran over. Khalid urged her to run away. We learned from the police report that Majors pointed his gun at her and said, "I'm going to fucking kill you." When the woman froze, Khalid yelled at her, "Go away!" The neighbor told us Khalid saved her life.

Rami: The ambulance arrived quickly, maybe four or five minutes later.

Victoria: Khalid died in the ambulance. They found Majors several hours later close by, just outside the local library. He was sitting on a hill.

Haifa: He killed a very innocent soul. Very innocent.

Victoria: Our world was shattered. My brother was murdered on the front porch of our home.

Haifa: He saved my life and my husband's life. The neighbor's, too. That monster would have killed us all.

Victoria: When I think of Khalid's murder, I don't think there is any one single cause. It was hate, prosecutorial and judicial incompetence, racism and bias, mental health, gun violence, and domestic violence. It was a terrible storm and it all resulted in my brother's murder.

Haifa: The neighbor hated us.

Victoria: He repeatedly attacked our ethnicity and perceived faith.

Haifa: He was hateful to anyone from a different background.

Victoria: He should have been charged with a hate crime after running over my mother. A hate crime charge was brought in the murder case, but under Oklahoma law, it is just a misdemeanor. The most serious charge is murder in the first degree. From my mom's perspective, it doesn't matter.

Haifa: Nothing will bring my son back. But if we were white, he would never have touched us. I truly believe that.

Victoria: But calling it a hate crime allows us to better tackle bigotry and hatred. It allows the public and media to see this crime not as isolated or random, but as part of a larger problem. Right after the tragedy, we received emails and calls from people describing how they felt hated by a neighbor or their community. An Iraqi woman with three children described how her neighbor kept harassing her family. We can't dismiss this tragedy as a one-off. Hate is why he attacked us rather than the other neighbors.

Rami: There were many reports covering the story that focused on Muslim-related slurs or hateful language towards Islam or Arabs. As Arab (Lebanese) Christians, we were sort of in a unique position. On the one hand we wanted the public to know that Khalid was an Orthodox Christian because it is important to our family's identity, but on the other hand this could have been perceived as us saying, "We are

Christian, not Muslim," or "Look, our family was not even Muslim." Regardless, none of this should matter. Our family, our mother, and our brother were targeted because we came from somewhere else; we were different. All forms of hate are equal and positively intolerable, whether it's targeting Muslims, Jews, Hindus, Sikhs, blacks, Asians, Hispanics, or other communities.

Victoria: We're in this struggle together. We never said, "Leave us alone. We're not Muslim."

Rami: I think Trump's dog-whistle rhetoric has made hate worse. Unlike leaders of prior administrations, Trump won't even condemn hate violence. He says little or nothing at all about hate crimes. Inaction is painful and damaging too. The year 2017 was the first in many decades that the White House didn't host an iftar dinner to celebrate Ramadan.

Victoria: They had an Easter celebration.

Rami: Exactly. That's intentional. They want to send a message that Muslims don't belong here. They don't want to celebrate Muslims and the contributions they've made to this country. They don't want to be inclusive.

Victoria: Some of his supporters say things like, *Now, it's our time. You had your time.*

Rami: It's like some of them want the old South to rise again, and keep America white and Christian only.

Victoria: They see a level playing field as a threat to the advantages and privileges they've long held. This administration is propagating fear. They want everyone to think that people who look different from them are out to get to them. I sometimes feel like we're in a civil war, us versus them. I also think there's a cultural sickness in America. I think about the lack of education, the stigma and lack of treatment of

mental illness, and the paucity of resources and social services. There's a lack of community. I think all of that contributed to Trump's election.

Haifa: The man next door had zero friends. Nobody. He even
abused his partner.

Victoria: My family is a part of so many communities—Lebanese,
Christians, Tulsans, and others. We're active in these communities, and it's the reason we were able to survive this
tragedy. The guy next door didn't have a community. Maybe he never did. Someone once emailed me, saying he was
Majors's cousin. He said Majors's mother abandoned him
when he was three months old, and that he lived in a car
with his dad growing up. I don't know if it's true. But the
point is that we have this cultural sickness and the only way
to combat it is through forging community.

Rami: I also think that in this case the system failed. Khalid's
death was preventable.

Victoria: This man was a known danger. He hated our family,
ran over my mother, and twice violated a protective order,
and they still let him out of jail. They put him next door to
us, the family he hated and assaulted, without any monitoring of any kind. No ankle monitor, no drug or alcohol testing, no nothing.

Rami: We protested and were vigilant in our communications
with the district attorney's office. If the "justice system"
didn't work for our family, a family who had two lawyers
following up and actively communicating with the DA's
office at every step, we can only assume the system is failing
so many others.

Victoria: The decision to release him on bond would have been
troubling at any time, but it was really disturbing given the
climate of our country and rising tide of hate violence. In

addition, only thirty minutes prior to my brother's shooting, Khalid called the police, saying this man had a gun and that he was scared. The police came and told him there was nothing to be done. Minutes later, our brother was murdered.

Haifa: They should have gone in. My son would still be alive today.

Victoria: I also think that if the neighbor wielding the gun had been black, Arab, or Muslim, the police would have found their way inside that home. I believe that with all my heart and soul.

Haifa: Yes, they would have entered.

Rami: Even without a warrant, they probably would have entered and invoked some exception to the warrant requirement which can be allowed under the law.

Victoria: In this case, he also had a criminal record and a history of bigotry. His white skin protected him.

Rami: The same could maybe be said for granting bond, too. If this monster had been black, Hispanic, or Middle Eastern and had that same history, I'm doubtful he would've been allowed to post bond.

Haifa: We also learned recently that the monster used to abuse Stephen.

Victoria: I think domestic violence also played a role. People who abuse their family and partners often abuse others.

Rami: There's also gun violence. I don't think anybody in our family has really ever held a gun. Now, my wife and I are part of a homicide support group in Dallas, where we live. All of the homicides were due to gun violence. We never wanted to be part of that group; nobody does. But being in the group helps.

Victoria: People have asked us why we didn't buy a gun to protect ourselves. We don't believe in guns. We shouldn't have
needed one to protect our family.

Rami: Today, I am trying to use my legal background to work
on bail and bond reform. It doesn't involve combating hate,
but it'll make this country a safer place. Dangerous people, like our neighbor, need to be kept off the streets and in
custody while they await trial, period. Non-dangerous or
simple low-level offenders, like most drug users who pose
no threat to the public and often suffer from mental health
issues, should be treated or admitted to a drug program, not
held in custody where they take up resources and space. It
sounds simple, but unfortunately in many states the system
is backwards.

Victoria: I think Rami and I have struggled to figure out how
we can help, given the terrible perfect storm of tragedies
that culminated in our brother's death. We're all trying to
find something we're interested in. I've been advocating for
Oklahoma to adopt some version of Marsy's Law, which has
been adopted in California and Illinois and is under consideration in several other states. The law provides additional
rights to victims of crime. For example, it allows victims to
be heard at every stage of a criminal proceeding, not just at
sentencing. It also gives victims the right to be represented
by their own counsel, rather than a prosecutor, whose obligations and incentives sometimes differ from victims'. This
law might have saved Khalid's life.

Rami: It also requires that victims be notified in advance of
all court proceedings. In our case, we checked the docket
almost every day and had to proactively reach out to the
district attorney's office. This law would require them and
the court to be in touch with us.

Victoria: I'm also doing a lot of education and interfaith work in my local community. I decided after Khalid's death that if we want love and understanding, we must start with our children. Yesterday, on July 7, 2017, on what would have been Khalid's 38th birthday, a library at my daughter's preschool in Tulsa, B'nai Emunah, was dedicated in his name. The Khalid Jabara Tikkun Olam Library contains children's books and family resources on justice, inclusion, diversity, and social change. *Tikkun Olam* is Hebrew for "repair the world." The wonderful work that will happen in the library will allow our children from birth through age six to have the vision to repair the world. It means so much to me that my daughter, Layla, will have a daily reminder of her loving uncle Khalid.

Rami: More than six hundred books were collected for the library in less than three weeks.

Victoria: I was thankful that the Tulsa Public Schools superintendent and the mayor of Tulsa spoke at the dedication yesterday. Think about it. An Arab mother took her daughter to a synagogue, where she learned Hebrew songs in a library dedicated to her Arab uncle. Now that's America.

When I think about Khalid today, what I miss most is his laughter and heart. Every Jabara family joke was his. He was so good at impersonations and accents. He was so loving to my daughter, his niece that he won't see grow up. I also know that he struggled a lot, just trying to be, and I'm sad he didn't get to experience life. He didn't get to enjoy it the way he deserved.

Rami: I'm married and want to have kids someday. Khalid will never get to meet them. He was so unique and charming. Everyone loved him. He always tried to help others. Even in his final minutes, he kept my mom, father, and neighbor away from near certain death.

Haifa: I know that he's gone, but I see him every day. I see him all the time. On the couch. In his room. I don't want to believe it. I can't believe it.

Victoria: My sweet brother had a heart of gold.

4

JEANETTE VIZGUERRA

*Trump has stripped away many of the rights of undocument-
ed immigrants and has intensified raids and deportations. He
classified every undocumented immigrant as a priority for
deportation; ordered state and local law enforcement to cooperate in detaining undocumented immigrants; expanded the
expedited removal program so that more immigrants could be
deported without seeing a judge; ended the Deferred Action
for Childhood Arrivals (DACA) program; and curtailed the
Temporary Protected Status (TPS) program. Trump has also
sought to punish sanctuaries by withholding funds to sanctuary jurisdictions, and has at times allowed immigration
authorities to enter and apprehend immigrants in sensitive
locations.*

*Jeanette Vizguerra is an undocumented organizer and activ-
ist who has fought for labor rights and immigration reform for
more than a decade. She is the mother of four and makes her*

home in Denver, Colorado. This interview was translated from
Spanish.

IN EARLY FEBRUARY, MY CHILDREN AND I GATHERED AROUND
our dinner table. I told them that men in uniform might come to
our home and take me away. Luna (who's twelve), Roberto (ten),
and Zury (six) looked at me and listened. They knew we were
different from other families. I'm undocumented, and they were
born here. The only way I could stay safe was to take sanctuary
at a local church and trust that the government would honor
the sanctity of the house of worship. Their father and my eldest
daughter, Tania, who's twenty-six, would take care of them.

I gave the children explicit instructions. If somebody knocked,
don't open the door. If somebody entered, Luna should film;
Roberto should run to the refrigerator and call the first person
on the community contact list; and Zury should run to the bedroom and close the door. I feared for their safety.

I didn't want to leave my family, but I was scared that Immigration and Customs Enforcement (ICE) would tear us apart.

When Trump was elected president, I knew that things would
be different. I had successfully advocated against many local and
state anti-immigrant laws, and found ways to resist and counter mass deportations during the Obama presidency. But under
Trump, we anticipated heightened force, detention, and deportation. Trump said that he would repeal DACA and build a wall,
calling us "bad hombres." I took him at his word.

I first caught the attention of immigration authorities in
2009, when I received a misdemeanor conviction for attempt-
ing to use a fake social security number. The IRS knows that
many undocumented workers earn wages, so they give us an
Individual Tax Identification Number (ITIN) to use when we
report our income. That way, they can collect taxes on billions
of additional dollars. But to get a job, we must first complete a
work authorization check, which requires a valid social secu-

government said that my case was under investigation. What could they be investigating? I had been in the U.S. for twenty years. I feared the worst.

Then I saw what happened to Guadalupe Garcia de Rayos in Arizona and Daniel Ramirez Medina in Washington just after Trump took office. Guadalupe had received numerous extensions from deportation after being convicted for using a fake social security number. Then, on February 8, she was detained and deported to Mexico. Two days later, on February 10, Daniel Ramirez Medina, a young man protected under DACA, was taken into custody and slated for deportation. I thought I was next.

I took sanctuary in the First Unitarian Society of Denver church on February 14, 2017. The church was active in anti–Vietnam War protests and the anti-nuclear movement, and resisted U.S. interventions abroad, including the Iraq War. Years ago, I had helped to design the room where I stayed, knowing that one day I might need it. We painted it white and yellow, my favorite colors. White means pure and yellow means hope. I still remember my youngest daughter getting paint all over her hair. The church also added a closet and bed. The congregation was an extension of my family. I will never forget their generosity and kindness.

For decades, immigration authorities have treated certain locations, like houses of worship, schools, and hospitals, as sensitive. These are honored community centers that shouldn't be policed. I wanted to protect my family and others in case my stay wasn't renewed, and so years earlier I helped create a sanctuary network in Denver. I went from church to church with my children, sharing our story. Many of the people I met were conservative and couldn't relate to my family. "Why should we give you space if you committed a crime?" they would ask. Some knew very little about our immigration system. When I described my reasons for immigrating, the story of my U.S.-born children, and all of my years living and contributing to this country, they understood my perspective. Many didn't even know that I paid

rity number. Undocumented immigrants buy these nur.
the street. It's another example of worker abuse. They
income, knowing that we use fake social security numbe.
then detain or deport us at will for using those numbers.

I received my second misdemeanor conviction in 201.
unlawfully entering the country. My mother was terminal,
in Mexico, and I wanted to pay my last respects. After a l
return journey back to the U.S., I was apprehended by Borc
Patrol in El Paso, Texas.

During my detention in El Paso, I feared that I would b,
deported and separated from my family, so I got in touch with
my community in Colorado from inside the detention center. I
told them who to call, who to pressure, and where to protest. We
worked day and night. Our persistence paid off. Although ICE
ordered my deportation, I was released under the supervision of
the government and permitted to leave voluntarily. I subsequent-
ly received five stays of removal, which temporarily halted the
deportation process. I was fortunate. Most immigrants never get
a second chance.

I had no intention of leaving. My family fled Mexico City in
1997 because of the terrible violence there. My husband was a
chauffeur and was the victim of three kidnappings. I feared for
Tania, who was six at the time. We settled in Denver because my
husband had family there.

The U.S. is my home. Three of my four children were born
here, and all of them are young. Even my Tania has no memory
of Mexico. She has a work permit under DACA and three children of her own. We pay taxes, contribute to the local economy,
and give back. There was nothing left for me in Mexico City
after my mother passed.

My general practice was to submit my stay application thirty days before expiration. But after Trump was elected, I took
additional precautions. I submitted my application sixty-nine
days before its date of expiration, February 15, 2017. Weeks
passed, and we heard nothing. When my lawyer inquired, the

taxes. We now have a coalition of nineteen churches, called the Metro Denver Sanctuary Coalition, that have agreed to serve as sanctuaries for undocumented immigrants.

I had a strong feeling on the day of my hearing that my request would be denied. My lawyer and my pastor attended on my behalf. When my pastor entered the government building, he messaged me and told me to stay away. There was a group of uniformed officers wearing black with heavy artillery, rather than the officer or two I was accustomed to seeing. Just a few minutes later, they rejected my application and ordered my arrest.

I wept. I thought I would be in sanctuary for four years, the entirety of the Trump administration. I was also angry. I was in a different space, outside of my home, and in unfamiliar surroundings. I wanted to be with my children. But it was my children who brightened my spirits. They reminded me that I was safe and supported by the community. They said they would be my voice and take to the streets, just as I would. They were right. I was living in sanctuary, not a jail cell.

Those were busy and difficult months. I had visitors almost every day, including family, friends, and the media. I gave presentations to students who visited the church and held know-your-rights workshops that were open to the public. My husband and eldest daughter took care of the children. They would visit me on the weekends. I longed to be with them.

When I was in sanctuary, I received immense hate because of my immigration status and Latina identity. People would call and send messages saying that I didn't belong in this country, I should go home, and there should be a wall. The most offensive and hurtful messages were about my children. I did my best to shield them from it all, but it wasn't possible because there was so much of it. People said I was exploiting my children to remain in the U.S. They called me a "dog" and said I should leave and take my "puppies" with me. They said they didn't want my children in this community or in their kids' schools. They said

I was abusing the system and exploiting public services. I was particularly shocked by that charge because I always took good care of my children. I never asked the government for anything.

I also received threats of violence, which I reported to the police. People even threatened to bomb the church and kill everyone inside. Never before had I seen, nor could I have imagined, such hate. I was scared for the congregation, and couldn't bear the idea of people being harmed because of me. Sometimes I feared for my children. Late at night, I would lie in bed and worry that they would be targeted. I would have left sanctuary to be with them if they were harmed. They're the most important things in my life.

Many of the messages and calls were from white supremacists. They often mentioned Trump. He continues to generate hate, racism, and discrimination against people of different races, faiths, and other diverse communities. He's opened the door for white supremacists to act on their prejudice and hurt others. There was little I could do from inside the church to resist, but I did my best. I cooperated with law enforcement. I also publicly exposed the profiles of those who sent me hateful or threatening messages. I wanted the community to know and share their profiles as well. Hate has no place in our community. Sometimes I even responded to the messages because it felt therapeutic and was a way of resisting. I had so few ways of engaging with the outside world.

I stayed at the First Unitarian Society church for two and a half months. I spent two additional weeks at the First Baptist Church, also located in Denver. After three months of sanctuary, I was granted a stay of removal until March 2019, thanks to private bills introduced by my elected officials in Congress. There is a longstanding practice to grant stays requested by elected officials. After my case and others, Trump abandoned this tradition.

Roughly eighteen months ago, I submitted an application for a U visa, which is intended for victims of crimes who have suffered mental or physical abuse and their family members. The hate and threats of violence that my family and I endured during sanctuary make my application even stronger. I want to eliminate the uncertainty of repeated stays and hearings. I want to live in this country for the rest of my life.

In the spring, just before leaving sanctuary, *Time* magazine named me one of 2017's "100 Most Influential People" in the world. They called me an icon. I took great pride in this honor because it showed the world that undocumented immigrants can earn distinguished titles. It also demonstrated that fighting for civil rights and racial justice is an achievement that should be honored. That award belongs to all undocumented immigrants. We're in this struggle together. Trump was also on the list, but the contrast couldn't be clearer. He fights for anger and hate; I fight for justice, dignity, and equality.

As I look ahead and think about immigration reform, I believe we must continue to educate and create consciousness. From the time I started organizing to the time I helped build the sanctuary network, I saw the biases that people have about immigrants, in particular undocumented immigrants: we don't work hard; we don't pay taxes; we drain public resources; we steal jobs; we're criminals. None of this is true. We work hard; we pay our share of taxes; we don't drain resources; we take jobs that others often refuse; and we do everything in our power to avoid law enforcement because we're immigrants. There was a brief period when my husband and I ran a small moving company, and we hired U.S. citizens. Even though we paid them above minimum wage, they lasted only a few weeks because the work was too difficult. We hired people; we didn't take their jobs away.

I've found that people are willing to listen if you share your story. Many thought I would fail as an organizer because my English skills were limited and I worked as a janitor. I later became one of the most successful organizers in the region. Many thought the sanctuary network would fail because the church membership was too conservative. We now have a large coalition because their membership learned that we contribute and care about the community just as they do. We have to lead by example and always educate.

Sometimes when I give school presentations, I ask the students if they recently moved to Denver. Many raise their hands. When I ask why they moved, they typically say better schools and jobs, and a higher quality of life. It's the same with immigrants, I tell them. They crossed a state line; we crossed a border. Boundaries are merely administrative decisions.

We must also focus on other civil rights issues that disproportionately impact immigrants. Immigrants experience immense discrimination and abuse in the workplace. I served as an organizer with the SEIU for many years, and saw this firsthand. Employers would pay immigrants less for the same work, verbally abuse and insult them, and force them to return to work, falsely claiming that they hadn't finished a job. When the workers would return, the employers would demand that they complete a different job or perform additional work. They would never pay for their additional time. Wage theft and firing without justification were commonplace.

Immigrants without papers, like me, had it the worst. We would have to work more than others and were disproportionately subject to wage theft and unfair firing. If we complained about our wages, employers would threaten to call the authorities or to fire us and withhold back pay. I heard stories of employers who would threaten entire families unless they provided free labor. All workers deserve strong protections in the workplace regardless of immigration status. All workers should belong to unions that will fight for their rights.

In addition, many immigrants don't have access to affordable education, housing, and health care. Why should we stay in the U.S. if we are a permanent underclass? I may be one of "The 100 Most Influential People" in the world, but I still don't have health insurance. I can't afford it, and I only visit the doctor when I have an emergency.

We must pressure Congress, too; otherwise, they'll hide behind Trump. It's the responsibility of Congress to regulate immigration. Trump said he would repeal DACA and he did; now Congress must pass a law to ensure that the Dreamers and others can stay. They must also encourage Trump to honor the sensitive locations policy. Hundreds of churches across the country have agreed to provide physical sanctuary to undocumented immigrants, and many already have. It's one of the primary ways we've resisted Trump's immigration agenda. But he may abandon the policy soon. It's already happening in some places. Although I can't vote, I continue to mobilize voters, especially in churches, to engage with their elected officials.

As I continue this work in the years ahead, I know that I will experience racism and hate. But I will press on because I want a better future for my children. I also know that one day I may be forced to leave this country. But it won't be without a fight. I will protect what I've earned and built. I will protect my family and the love and community we enjoy. And if I am deported, I will hold my head up high. From the day I arrived more than twenty years ago, I've fought for what I believed. My children will continue this fight long after I'm gone.

This is our home.

5

ALEXANDRA BRODSKY

Alexandra Brodsky is a civil rights attorney, a co-founder of Know Your IX, and a fellow at the National Women's Law Center (NWLC), where she works on education equity and school discipline issues.

IN THE DAYS FOLLOWING THE ELECTION, I STAFFED A NATIONAL hotline run by the NWLC through which students and families could report incidents of discrimination in school. We heard a similar story time after time. Girls were being groped on the playground by boys claiming that if the president could do it, so could they. In a 2017 report, NWLC reported that more than one in six girls ranging in age from fourteen to eighteen had experienced harassment since Trump's election. Women aren't safe in schools, workplaces, public life, or online.

Boys and men across the country are parroting the president. Many men—white men in particular—have long believed that they are entitled to the bodies of others. This manifests in the form of gender violence, domestic violence, and even the shooting of young black men. The election of Donald Trump reaffirmed this belief and made it infectious and viral.

On the campaign trail, Trump insulted the bodies of women, engaged in sexual harassment, and bragged about sexual assault. He berated women for being overweight. He repeatedly talked about women bleeding, calling to mind historical tropes about women being hysterical and incapacitated by their hormones and emotions. I'm no fan of Megyn Kelly, but I was disgusted that Trump wants to disqualify women from political life because they menstruate. During the presidential debates, he stood over Hillary Clinton, interrupted her, and followed her around the stage. When she resisted, he dismissed her as a "nasty woman." The unearthing of the 2005 *Access Hollywood* recording confirmed what many of us had long suspected. Trump is proud of having committed sexual assault.

I've fought against gender violence since college. I was sexually assaulted during my freshman year at Yale. Sexual violence wasn't an abstract issue; it was my story, too. Again and again, the school administration failed to respond adequately to private reports of sexual violence and mass incidents of sexual harassment on campus. These incidents included students marching around the freshman quad yelling, "No means yes" and "Yes means anal"; blocking the entrance to the women's center on campus, which also served as a rape crisis center; and interfering with a T-shirt campaign, where survivors shared their stories on T-shirts. Men would steal the T-shirts and wear them to discredit the survivors' stories. When the school remained unresponsive, fifteen classmates and I filed a Title IX complaint with the Department of Education.

Title IX is a critical civil rights law that prohibits sex discrimination in educational institutions that receive federal funding. Schools are required under the law to respond to reports of sexual harassment, including sexual assault, to investigate complaints, to ensure a safe environment, and to provide accommodation to survivors. Gender violence is not just a crime. It's also a civil rights issue. You can't learn when you're sharing a library with someone who harassed you. You can't focus in class when you're sharing a dorm with an abusive ex-partner.

I soon realized that students nationwide were encountering similar issues and that we needed institutional memory for our movement, so my friend Dana Bolger and I started Know Your IX, a youth-led movement to fight gender violence in schools.

When I think about Trump's election, I see a paradox. His campaign and victory mobilized people to condemn gender violence, but it was also a vote of national approval. The work of survivors and advocates allowed us to recognize the gender violence that Trump was admitting and promoting. Ten years ago, if a candidate mentioned kissing women without their consent, there wouldn't have been immediate mass recognition that he was talking about sexual assault. We have a better vocabulary and understanding of gender violence today than we did before.

But people voted for him anyway. It's both true that there has been incredible mobilization but also that we haven't won yet. Male supremacy is very important to many people's understanding of the world and their place within it. Yes, sexual violence affects people of all genders and people of all genders perpetrate it, but men are the vast majority of perpetrators. There are plenty of men—rich white ones in particular—who believe they can touch women as they please. Having someone in power like Trump returns and confirms their privilege.

White men have been afforded extraordinary privileges in this country and feel threatened by a more level playing field. The mass political mobilization and major progress we've made on civil rights and women's liberation feel like injustices to them. They feel like something has been taken away, and indeed it has: their supremacy has been questioned.

White women also have much to reckon with because a majority of us voted for Trump. As a group, we've repeatedly made the choice to prioritize protection of white men on the basis of our shared whiteness over our own liberation and that of others.

I experienced the new normal in Trump's America in February 2017. I was viciously cybertrolled for being a gender violence survivor, an outspoken feminist activist, and because of my Jewish faith. Images of me were photoshopped in disturbing ways and disseminated online. In one, they added the Star of David; in another, they transposed my face onto a lamp shade. The Star of David was the one Jews were required to wear in Nazi-occupied countries during WW II; the lamp shade was a clear reference to the Nazi practice of making lamp shades out of the skin of Jewish people. The attacks were politically inspired. The messages said things like, "This is Trump's country now," and "Welcome to Trump's America. See you in the camps!"

Dana, my co-founder at Know Your IX, also received vicious messages saying things like, "Don't think you're off the hook. We know your co-founder is a Jew." Current employees and volunteers at Know Your IX received similar messages as well. Soon thereafter, I learned that another woman named Alexandra Brodsky received emails intended for me saying similar things, like, "This is Trump's country now"; "See you in the concentration camps"; and "You'll be dead soon." My friends, colleagues, and a namesake were terrorized because of their proximity to me.

I know the harassment pales in comparison to the violence so many have faced since the election. But I'll be honest: I was shaken. Harassment that uses personal images is particularly scary because it feels like a person has access to you and control over you. The fact that it was online was also difficult because you never know how seriously to take it. I tried to brush it off but was relieved when my employer, NWLC, talked to a cyber-security firm and informed building security about the matter.

By that point I'd been writing about feminist issues on the internet for a few years. I knew that marginalized people—especially those who dare to speak up—are disproportionately subject to online harassment, cybertrolling, and other forms of intimidation. Trolls refuse to engage with us on the merits of our ideas, so they resort to abuse, misogyny, or worse. I was likely targeted by individuals who were hostile to women, gender violence survivors, and Jews. There's a stereotype that women lie about rape for personal benefit, and there's another that Jews are sneaky and play the role of victim even when we're in control. I sat at the intersection of those myths. Being an active feminist writer and organizer only intensified that hate.

I consider myself a Reform Jew. I was bat mitzvahed, went to Hebrew school, and celebrated Shabbat as a child. My Jewish identity is both cultural and religious, and remains a strong part of my family identity. Although I don't express my faith publicly very often, it was painful to be targeted in part because of it. Trump has intensified anti-Semitism in America. Cemeteries have been desecrated, and the ranks of neo-Nazis continue to rise. The president has seemed reluctant to even acknowledge that Jews were murdered in the Holocaust.

What makes it worse is that some Jews voted for Trump and chose their whiteness over their faith. Many said that they were willing to overlook Trump's failures because he could still do the job better than Hillary could, or because—for reasons I don't understand—they thought he'd be more supportive of Israel. That's privilege. Many communities can't afford to ignore misogyny or hate. In the aftermath of the harassment against me, I sent the images to a family member who voted for Trump, but he never responded.

When activists are harassed online, we often dismiss it as an inevitable part of online life. I think that's dangerous. The targeted have the greatest contributions to make to our policies and politics, and often they will speak out only if they feel safe and protected from harassment.

I fought back in the small way I could. I reported the abusive users to Twitter and shared screenshots of the images with my followers, with a simple comment: "Happy Saturday In Trump's America." I wanted both to pressure Twitter to suspend the abusive users and to make visible the new normal in Trump's America. Two days later, Twitter suspended my account. I was notified that I had to delete my tweet with the screenshots to unlock my account. The accounts of those who harassed me were still online and active.

I immediately complained about my treatment on Facebook and contacted some of my friends in journalism, who made inquiries with Twitter. The media took note, and a few outlets, including CNN, covered the story. Twitter reversed its decision and reinstated my account later that day. But public and widespread criticism shouldn't be a prerequisite to stop online harassment. I was lucky to have friends in media who could help. But what about the Title IX youth organizers in schools? Or the black girls trolled by white supremacists?

Many feminist writers no longer use social media because their online abusers have threatened their families or, worse, shown up on their doorstep. I continue to use social media because it's important for my work. Twitter is an excellent tool for information dissemination, organizing, and understanding the opposition. But when I write or tweet something, I now weigh the cost of the ensuing harassment. I hope I'm never forced to abandon social media altogether.

Many girls' entire middle- or high-school experience will be under the Trump presidency, and their lives will be fundamentally altered because of it. Recently, the Department of Education rescinded important policies about Title IX and sexual harassment that the last administration had published. In its place, the department put out "guidelines" that encourage schools to tilt the scales in favor of accused rapists and to roll back survivors' rights. They even got rid of important language about the importance of schools providing victims with services and support, like mental health care and tutoring. Plus, the

Trump administration has rolled back systemic investigations into sexual harassment and also other issues, like school discipline and racism in schools. Previously, one individual's incident could prompt a broader probe or a pattern investigation. Now that won't happen because the administration prefers a more narrow approach to civil rights enforcement. If we look only at individual cases, we miss the broader, systemic problem.

Advocates' engagement with government officials has been fraught, to say the least. In July 2017, the Department of Education's top official tasked with enforcing Title IX protections expressed skepticism about the vast majority of survivors' claims. In an interview with the *New York Times*, Candice Jackson, the head of the education department's civil rights office, said that 90 percent of sexual assault claims were fabricated.[1] The very next day, survivors of sexual violence and representatives of organizations like NWLC met with Secretary of Education Betsy DeVos for the first time in the White House. That same day, DeVos also met with groups like the National Coalition For Men, a "men's rights" group that publishes the names and photos of survivors to facilitate harassment. Their presence was abominable. Survivors and misogynists are not two equally valid sides of this fight.

But we've fought back. The NWLC sued the Department of Education, seeking information about active Title IX matters, because we don't think they're enforcing the law. On the day of the meeting, outside the Education Department, we helped to stage a protest that centered survivors. We're also educating girls and women about their rights and helping them engage with policymakers and elected officials, both locally and nationally. Girls and women nationwide spoke up and helped defeat the repeal of the Affordable Care Act. NWLC and our partners sent a letter to every state in the country demanding that trans students continue to be protected under Title IX after Attorney General Jeff Sessions issued guidance suggesting otherwise.

History tells us that local solutions can never fully replace federal ones, because people will always be left behind. Federal law will always be an important backstop. But we should nevertheless focus our energy on building local communities that can create local solutions. Faith communities, university organizations, and schools have all stepped up. We need to continue to leverage these institutions and communities, and remember that we're not starting from scratch. Advocates and organizers have been fighting gender violence and anti-Semitism for a long time.

When I was in school, I remember survivors expressing trepidation about coming forward because they feared that their abusers would retaliate. Their abusers were wealthy white boys or young men whose parents could seek legal counsel and quickly attack the reputation of a survivor and discredit her story. They feared speaking out because their abusers could be the congressmen, senators, CEOs, or presidents of tomorrow. The campaign and victory of Donald Trump confirmed their worst suspicions.

knives had been stabbed into the table and a noose was hanging from the ceiling.

I was devastated, scared, and angry. I didn't know what to think. I was immediately scared for the safety of everybody in the organization. Our space had been violated. For many of us, especially our youth volunteers, the office is our second home. Many of us feared for our safety. That's what happens when your home is violated. Every time you're there, you remember the violation. You remember that people who wished you harm walked the same ground. I get emotional every time I talk about it because although nothing was stolen, they sent us a message: *Stop the work you're doing. Stop speaking truth.*

I was born in Khao I Dang, a Cambodian refugee camp in Thailand. My family fled Cambodia during the civil war and settled in Revere, Massachusetts. I later moved to Rhode Island, where I co-founded PrYSM more than seventeen years ago. I became a community organizer because I saw the violence and injustice facing Southeast Asians in America and wanted to build greater solidarity among my people and all people.

From its inception to today, our organization's base has consistently been Southeast Asian young people. By Southeast Asian, I mean people from the countries of Cambodia, Laos, and Vietnam—the communities that became refugees after the Vietnam War, what we call the American War. My family were farmers in Cambodia when the genocide broke out. That's one base; those are our roots.

Another base is queer, transgender youth of color—black and brown youth who are not straight, not cisgendered. Their community desperately needs resources, support, and understanding. Plus, they mobilize and get work done! Many of the founders, myself included, also identify as queer, so it was a natural fit.

Survivors of state violence are our third base. One of the original callings of the organization was to fight our inclusion in the gang database of the Providence Police Department. We then launched a national campaign against the deportation of Cambodians liv-

6

SARATH SUONG

Sarath Suong is a co-founder and executive director of the Providence Youth Student Movement (PrYSM), an organization supporting Southeast Asians that seeks to eliminate state, street, and interpersonal violence.

It was December 2016. PrYSM had just celebrated its fifteenth anniversary over the weekend, and the staff and community were energized and excited. Although Trump had just won the election, we were pushing back and leading a major campaign to pass the Community Safety Act, a landmark city ordinance that would protect our communities and help ensure police accountability. But our sentiments quickly changed just two days later when we arrived at the office. We opened the door and saw that the furniture, office supplies, and eating utensils had been rearranged; the cabinet doors and desk drawers had been left wide open; and in the community room, two large ing in America, and later Lao and Vietnamese in America. Now we have a community defense project where we support survivors of police brutality and their families, and help them obtain legal recourse, mental health support, and police accountability.

In cities like Providence, these three demographics—Southeast Asian young people, trans/queer people of color, and survivors of state violence—are ignored, under-resourced, and targeted by the state and public. We provide these communities with services, give them support, and help them organize so that their voices are centered in city and state politics. Today PrYSM has a full-time staff of three and twenty organizers and volunteers. Our membership is in the thousands.

Our first priority as a young organization was to build a political narrative for Southeast Asians. That was easy because we all rallied around the same experience: U.S. militarism in our home countries. The U.S. had no moral or legal justification for invading our countries, other than "stopping Communism." They dropped more bombs in our countries than they did in the two world wars combined, and there are still bombs in the countryside in Cambodia, Laos, and Vietnam.

If U.S. militarism connected us, the gang database organized us. The wars in Southeast Asia caused one of the largest mass refugee flows in world history, and prompted the U.S. to create the Office of Refugee Resettlement. Many of us had no choice but to settle in the land of the invader. Worse, we were often resettled across the country and separated from our own extended families. The U.S. didn't want any single city or state to bear a "disproportionate number" of refugees.

Beginning in the 1980s and continuing through the 1990s, we started to form little enclaves, from Boston and Seattle to Long Beach and Philadelphia. The majority of us had been farmers and had limited language and professional skills. (The professional class in our countries, like teachers and doctors, were the first victims of the genocide.) We needed support from the U.S. government but never got it.

We had to fend for ourselves. We were a new immigrant community, looked different, and had been dumped into pockets of poverty across the country. Our elders had nightmares in the middle of the night; our older siblings were shell-shocked by the deaths they had seen; and the rest of us were babies and kids, just trying to grow up in a foreign land. The white kids would beat us up, and everyone else would bully us.

We came together in the streets. That's where we found community. That's where we found love. But the government saw a threat and called us gangs. The Providence Police Department then created a gang database to survey and monitor our daily lives.

I remember the moment when my peers and I started coming of age and we all realized that the police were an active presence in our lives. Even the honor roll kids, "the good kids," knew the police officers by name. I was shocked by that. I definitely wasn't on any honor roll. My friends would say, "We see them every day. They roll through our neighborhoods. They take pictures while we're out. They take pictures while we're on our porches. They randomly stop us and ask for our names."

That's how the police built the gang database. They would gather information about our community, and put our names, pictures, and associations into their database. Then we'd be "randomly" stopped and questioned, and the Providence police would know all about our lives. We weren't lawyers, but we knew this wasn't right. We started coming together. We started asking questions. We started wondering—could we dismantle the gang database?

PrYSM's very first meetings and conversations took place in my living room. It was friends and concerned community members who came at first. But we later grew into a much larger organization and began work on other anti-criminalization campaigns. In 2002, the U.S. had forced Cambodia to sign a repatriation agreement, which made a lot of Cambodian refugees eligible for deportation. Massachusetts had the second-largest Cambodian community in the country, and we actively fought against detention and deportation in our neighboring state. Today we are part of the End Displacement National Campaign, which seeks to end mass detention and deportation of immigrants. Under President Obama, two million immigrants were deported, 250,000 of whom were Asian American Pacific Islander. That's our community. We're fighting back.

We also work closely with queer and transgender youth in our community because they are particularly marginalized and misunderstood. In July 2012, we helped write and publish the very first report on LGBTQI Southeast Asians. "A Census of Our Own: The State of QSEA America" was a call to action to movement-builders and social change advocates to combat racism, homophobia, genderphobia, and economic oppression against LGBTQI Southeast Asians.

Our work with survivors of police violence is growing as well. We recently launched the Community Defense Project, a program that provides a variety of services to community members who have experienced police brutality. We have a community lawyer on staff who files administrative complaints against police officers and sues the police department. We also train and educate community members on Copwatch, a neighborhood watch program which monitors the police.

From our inception, we always recognized that our liberation was tied to others'. This country was founded on the genocide of indigenous communities and the slavery of black people. Our liberation required their liberation, too. That's why we've been quick to join struggles like Black Lives Matter and the resistance to the Dakota Access Pipeline.

We're fearless in Providence. We're not apologetic. We know what state violence does to our communities. We know what police violence does to our communities. We know what our community needs and how to get it. People have eyes on us. That's why we were the target of the hate crime in December 2016.

Immediately after our office was broken into, I started having flashbacks and remembering all the times that community members had been profiled and targeted by violence—state violence, street violence, and interpersonal violence. I had flashbacks of surveillance. I remembered when we would protest and the police would take our pictures. I remembered when staff would get pulled over by police for no reason at all. I remembered when I was pulled over for no reason at all, other than that I'm the director of an organization that wants to keep law enforcement honest. But this felt different.

We immediately created a safety plan. The physical and emotional safety of our staff, youth, and other communities who use our space was our top priority. We got the locks changed, secured the windows with wooden sticks, and locked the computers. Until further notice, nobody was allowed to be in the office alone. Staff had to check in and out using a group chat on our phones. If one of us was going to the office, all of us had to be on notice. We also decided to monitor the office through a neighborhood watch program and for all staff to take self-defense classes.

We felt like refugees again. We needed to be insular and to protect each other. But it was a delicate balance. Our space means so much to so many people, and in the end it doesn't belong to us, it belongs to the community. So, we quietly regrouped from the traumatic violation and took safety precautions, while keeping our space as open as possible. Some weeks later, we convened an open meeting with community members to hear their ideas on how we should move forward. We tried to be as collaborative as possible.

Our principles were really put to the test. Many of our supporters wanted us to install cameras and an alarm system in the office. This was a serious decision, as heightened security measures like cameras would undermine our principle of decreasing surveillance of already heavily policed communities. We decided against surveillance and rejected the use of all cameras.

Our youth are surveilled everywhere they go, and we refused to adopt that culture at PrYSM.

We also decided not to call the police. We are an abolition organization and believe in the abolition of the police and military. Think of it this way. We came to this country because of U.S. militarism. Then we got here and were targeted by state violence, like surveillance, the school-to-prison pipeline, police brutality, mass incarceration, and even deportation back to our home countries. The police and military pose the greatest threat to our safety and dignity. So why should we call them in our time of need?

If abolition was one of our values, we had to stick to it in this moment. That's why calling the police wasn't an option. In that sense, the hate crime gave us an opportunity to reaffirm our values and principles, an opportunity to remind the world about who we are and what we stand for.

It wasn't easy. We were accused of lying about the incident, all because we didn't call the police. From the time we're young, we're taught that the police are our saviors. That only they can protect us and "stop crime." At PrYSM, we try to imagine and create a different world. In July 2017, for example, some computers were stolen from our office. While we could have called the police, we decided to handle it internally with the support of our community. We knew that most robberies are committed by people you know, and so we reached out to the PrYSM family, seeking information about the incident. In just a few days, we found the person responsible. He was suffering from drug addiction and made a mistake. Instead of punishing him, we helped him get the resources he needed.

We issued a public statement about the hate crime because the community and public had to know what happened. They all had to bear witness. We also wanted to show that we would not be intimidated and nothing would dampen our spirit. Their hate motivated us more. The noose is a tool of white supremacist terror, and so we also used that moment to recommit ourselves to the movement for black lives in Providence, the U.S., and globally.

We said nothing to the media. My primary concern was the safety and mental well-being of our organizers, young people, and the PrYSM family. The media couldn't help with that, so we decided against engagement.

When I think about why we were targeted, I can't divorce it from the politics of today. Racism and hate are now out in the open. It used to be that people were at least politically correct or mindful of the rights of others to exist. But not anymore. Those same people act with impunity. They say and do the most hateful things. And why not? If the leader of our country does, why can't they?

In that way, the attack on our office wasn't an isolated incident. It's part of a broader pattern of systemic injustice, racism, and policing of our bodies and ideas. The vandalism of mosques and Islamic centers, explicit homophobia, aggressive deportation campaigns targeting undocumented immigrants, restrictions on refugee admissions, and the revival of anti-abortion politics reflect just a sampling of these policies. Anti-black racism, Islamophobia, xenophobia, transphobia, homophobia, misogyny, anti-Semitism and anti-immigrant sentiment will all continue to grow in the Trump era, and so will hate violence.

It's important, though, not to give President Obama a pass. The deportation of our communities happened under Obama, too. Obama created a well-oiled, perfect deportation machine that he handed over to this administration. So, for us, it's been business as usual. The same foes, just a different face. We never had any illusions about Obama or any of his predecessors. There's a larger system, divorced from presidents and even political parties, that disenfranchises and targets us.

Sometimes it's hard, and we want to be more insular and closed off from the outside world. It's a feeling that refugees know well because we've lived it. But we have to resist that impulse because we need to be reaching out to others even more. We need to build campaigns that span multiple communities and protect us all.

We used the anger and frustration of the election and hate crime as motivation to do that. In June, after a grueling campaign that spanned five years, the City of Providence passed the most comprehensive anti-racial-profiling legislation in the country. The Community Safety Act was modeled after its namesake, passed in New York in 2013. The bill has twelve key provisions, relating to profiling, data collection, video recording by police, video recording by people, traffic stops, consent searches, surveillance, the privacy of youth and immigrants, gang lists, language access, collaboration with law enforcement agencies, and accountability and enforcement. It's not just the law, it's how we got there. Lawyers wrote the bill with the input of young people from our community, those most impacted by state violence.

I'm particularly proud that the law restores due process rights to those on gang lists, and prohibits the Providence police department from collaborating with federal agencies like ICE. Providence is now a true sanctuary city. In addition, there are important provisions that allow for transgender people and gender-non-conforming people to choose the gender of the officers searching them.

The Community Safety Act, and the process by which we got there, speaks to the nature of PrYSM as an organization. We were intersectional long before it became fashionable. It was a principle from our inception. We're survivors of state violence, queer and Southeast Asian. Our ranks are intersectional.

But we must remember that legislation won't save us. Nor will policy. Only community will. We must remain focused on organizing and community resilience. That's the pathway to collective liberation. That's how we build an enduring resistance.

7

MARWAN KREIDIE AND SHAHID HASHMI

In December 2015, Trump announced his intention to ban Muslims from entering the United States. He made true on this promise in January 2017, when he signed the first iteration of the Muslim and refugee ban, banning nationals from seven Muslim-majority countries and refugees from entering the United States.

Marwan Kreidie is a longtime Arab American activist, and the spokesperson for the Al-Aqsa Islamic Society mosque in Philadelphia. Shahid Hashmi is the president of the Victoria Islamic Center in Victoria, Texas, and one of the original members of the local Muslim community there.

Marwan Kreidie: On the morning of Monday, December 7, 2015, I went to the Al-Aqsa Islamic Society mosque in Philadelphia, and the caretaker ran up to me and said, "You won't believe what happened—someone threw a pig's head at the mosque."

"What? What are you talking about?"

"Yes! Someone threw a pig's head at the mosque."

It was the heart of primary season, and Muslims and Arabs were being scapegoated everywhere I turned. Two weeks earlier, then candidate Trump had publicly advocated for a federal database to track Muslims—a Muslim registry. We then heard rumblings on Sunday, the day before, that Trump was going to propose banning Muslims from the U.S. The very next day he did just that, calling for a "total and complete shutdown of Muslims entering the United States."[1] He later made true on that promise with different versions of the Muslim and refugee ban.

The community believed we were targeted because of Trump's comments and policies about Muslims, including the proposed ban. The mosque was my place of work and a religious and community center. I was really concerned. I called the police, FBI, and media. This time it was a pig's head. What would it be next time?

The police weren't able to apprehend the suspect because our security cameras were not sophisticated enough to capture important details. We don't think it was anyone from the neighborhood. There were reports of a red pickup truck driving around town that night, and police think the passengers may have attended a private, racist hard-rock concert. There's a circuit of these bands around the country, and their membership swells with neo-Nazis and white supremacists. They were probably having a pig roast and thought it would be nice to terrorize the local Muslim and Arab community.

Pork is considered non-halal, or food that is forbidden in Islam. A lot of people think it's kryptonite to Muslims, but it's not. The pig's head was meant to intimidate us.

The police are investigating the case. I think they desperately want to find the suspect because it would be a feather in their cap. The mosque leadership said they had forgiven the suspect just hours after the incident, but not me. There have been dozens of cases of mosques being vandalized and Korans being desecrated in recent years. Law enforcement needs to set an example. I don't think the suspect necessarily has to go to jail for a long time, but there should be a public trial and he should pay for his crimes, including perhaps community service and serving the community he harmed.

The response from elected officials was strong. Mayor-elect Jim Kenney called on the city residents to condemn the act of hate violence and support the Muslim and Arab community. Outgoing mayor Michael Nutter famously remarked after Trump pledged to ban Muslims that Philadelphia should ban Trump. These were important statements of support and they gave the community comfort during this difficult time.

The Al-Aqsa Islamic Society was formed in 1989. It was originally an offshoot of an older Albanian mosque located a few blocks away that had become overcrowded. The local community got a warehouse, secured a permit, and expanded it into what you see today. I now serve as the spokesperson for the mosque, a position I've held since 2000.

A few months before the incident, I remember talking to community members and saying it was worse than after 9/11. That was a very difficult time for the Muslim and Arab community because we feared a backlash. I thought people would throw rocks or break the windows of the mosque.

Instead, the reaction was one of support. People came to us and asked how they could help. They knew our pain, and that we had nothing to do with 9/11. I remember interfaith allies from a local synagogue and church coming to the mosque after the first Friday prayer after 9/11 and offering to take the women with hijabs shopping if they felt uncomfortable leaving their homes. I was really grateful; it was reassuring to have their support.

Fast-forward to today and, though we were worried something might happen given the political environment, we somehow thought we were immune. I think most community members saw the pig's head incident as an aberration, but many are still afraid and wonder what could happen next time.

We worry. We have to worry. We all agree that the Trump era has empowered people to embrace bigotry and commit acts of hate violence. Most people, including myself, believe we should prepare for the worst and hope for the best. I remember how upset my family was after the incident. I have three children: two teenage daughters and one teenage son. Just prior to the incident, we had discussed how racism and bigotry were on the rise. Then this happened. We agreed that it was an attack on us all.

The phrase "words have consequences" comes to mind. So many candidates were peddling xenophobic and anti-Muslim rhetoric at the time, including Trump, that I think the rhetoric spurred people to act out. The rhetoric reinforces preexisting bigotry and bias. It's really damaging. We've worked hard to fight hate in America, and now racists and bigots feel emboldened.

It's not just Trump's words; it's his policies, too. He promised to create a registry of Muslims living in America, vowed to ban Muslims from entering the U.S., and proposed to move the U.S. embassy in Israel from Tel Aviv to Jerusalem, thereby erasing any Palestinian claim to Jerusalem. Registering Americans and banning foreign nationals on account of faith? That's un-American.

I remember the National Security Entry–Exit Registration System that was created immediately after 9/11. It required persons residing temporarily in the U.S. from twenty-five predominately Muslim- or Arab-majority countries to register with the U.S. government. They faced invasive questioning, fingerprinting, and check-ins. They were targeted solely on account of their faith and national origin. I worry that Trump may create a similar system or perhaps a more expansive one.

He may also try to designate the Muslim Brotherhood a terrorist organization as a way to target Muslim and Arab charities and public-interest organizations in the U.S. One of the favorite smear tactics of anti-Muslim advocacy groups and hate mongers is to accuse Muslim and Arab activists, organizations, and their allies of supporting the Brotherhood. The accusation alone can destroy a reputation. It could be a witch hunt, just like the McCarthy era.

What Trump says about Mexicans and our Latinx brothers and sisters is just as bad. Philadelphia is a sanctuary city. We prohibit police officers from asking about the immigration status of people they encounter.

Immigrants come to this country seeking a better life and sometimes just want to reunite with their families. More undocumented immigrants live in Philadelphia than in any northeastern American city, except New York. Plus, many of our families are mixed, meaning some family members are documented, but others are not.

Now Trump wants to withhold federal funding to sanctuary cities. He also rescinded the Deferred Action for Childhood Arrivals order, which allowed undocumented immigrants who entered the country as minors to receive two-year periods of deferred action from deportation. Waging war on the undocumented community hurts the social, cultural, and economic fabric of our society. I want the mosque to become a sanctuary for undocumented persons. I think that's the obligation of every religious institution right now.

Some of us see and feel hate every day. I talked to a Christian Syrian who has a shop in the Reading Terminal Market and he told me that customers often avoid him now and give him bad looks. It's impacting his business. The Reading Terminal Market is a Philadelphia institution, and tourists go there from all over the state. If this is happening in a tolerant city like Philadelphia, imagine what's happening elsewhere.

I'm worried that some in our community will go back into the shadows because they fear for their safety. But we can't do that. Now is the time to talk, educate, engage, and organize. We need to partner with allies and step outside our comfort zone. That's what I plan to do.

I've been an organizer and activist for as long as I can remember. In the early 1980s, after college, I was very active on Palestinian issues. I did volunteer work to help Arab Americans, and in the late 1990s, I learned of the Al-Aqsa mosque and started a secular Arab American organization, called the Arab American Community Development Corporation (AACDC). We housed the organization in the mosque because the mosque is the largest Arab institution in Philadelphia. Although we're a secular organization, that's where we would have the largest reach and impact.

Mosques in America are like churches and other houses of worship. They're community centers, where we learn, organize, and thrive. This mosque is 90 percent Arab immigrant. The December attack wasn't just an attack on Muslims. It was an attack on Arabs and immigrants as well.

Our initial mandate at AACDC was land acquisition for the mosque. But 9/11 changed everything. We opened a food pantry, and started doing English classes and know-your-rights teach-ins. We focused on the most vulnerable in our community, primarily low-income and first-generation immigrant Arab families.

It's fair to say that I differed from others at the time because I thought Muslims and Arabs had to be vocal and active. Many wanted to stay in the shadows and were concerned about a possible backlash. I thought the backlash would intensify if we remained silent.

So I did my best to make sure our civil rights were protected, while simultaneously condemning the 9/11 attacks. It's a delicate balance as, ever since then, Muslims and Arabs have been asked to condemn acts of terrorism around the world. It's as though we have to prove our innocence day in and day out. No other community shoulders that burden. Nor should we.

Just as I did after 9/11, I will push back against the politics of today through organizing and coalition-building, especially in the interfaith community and with progressive allies. I co-founded a group called United Voices, which represents vulnerable communities in Philadelphia and, in particular, immigrants. We speak together with one voice.

In connection with that group, and other work, we organize those directly impacted by bigotry and state violence and hold forums and conversations where they share their stories. This allows us to build community and educate others about who we are and what we experience. With their counsel and support, we also advocate on their behalf with local and federal officials and invite them to meet with legislators. We are particularly active on issues relating to hate violence, immigration enforcement, sanctuary cities, the Muslim and refugee bans, and First Amendment protections, including free speech, association, and worship.

I remain particularly sensitive to the needs of low-income community members and recent immigrants. Because of their socio-economic status and limited language skills, they are at heightened risk of harassment, deprivation, and civil rights violations. We often partner with national advocacy groups like the Arab American Institute and the American Civil Liberties Union and hold know-your-rights teach-ins on free speech, expression, and worship, and on best practices when encountering law enforcement.

We are always committed to solidarity. It's not enough that Muslims and Arabs survive this administration. All communities must thrive. If there's a bill that helps interfaith communities but hurts the undocumented community, we must reject it. We must reject all piecemeal advocacy.

Philadelphia's growing diversity is a real opportunity. The city has changed a lot during my time here. It's gone from mostly black and white to a city with large Latinx, Asian, and Arab communities. These communities are now a critical part of the mosaic that is Philadelphia. Philadelphia gives me hope because it's a progressive city with an organized community. Muslims and Arabs should never feel alone in this city. Everyone I know says that if there is a Muslim registry, they'll register as Muslims.

Yet even so, I still can't wrap my head around what's happened. The anti-immigrant, anti-Arab, anti-Muslim, and xenophobic sentiments of today are unlike anything I've seen in my lifetime. 9/11 was a scary time and the aftermath was awful. But there's a huge difference between then and now. There was an attack on 9/11, and we knew there would be a backlash. What we've experienced recently, on the other hand, was the lead-up to and aftermath of a legitimate election. We elected Trump as president. We elected his rhetoric, policies, and cabinet. I still struggle with how anyone could have voted for him. Even my home state, Pennsylvania, voted for him.

Sometimes I can't help but think: *Why am I in this country now? Should I move elsewhere? Do I want to raise my kids in this country, where hate is so visible and rampant?* I've been in this fight for decades, but even I struggle. Deep down, though, I know we need to stay the course and continue the fight.

Looking back, what stands out the most about the hate crime wasn't the pig's head. It was the community's response. That same day, neighbors called me and said they wanted to come to the mosque after Friday prayer and hold a demonstration in support of the community. They wanted signs, speakers, speeches, megaphones, and a list of demands.

I said no to a demonstration and suggested a party instead. They agreed, and the following Saturday, we had four to five hundred people at the mosque, including rabbis, pastors, elected officials, and neighbors, and we built community together. The neighbors cared, and they showed it that day. They were just as upset as we were, and did everything they could to rebuild the trust that was shattered. It was an amazing celebration of life.

Food, community, and love is how we condemned hate. It was our way of showing the world that hate wouldn't be tolerated in the City of Brotherly Love. It was the best of Philadelphia. The pig's head didn't divide us; it brought us together.

Shahid Hashmi: The summer of 2002 was a special time for our family. Arooj, my eldest child, got married at our local mosque. My wife and I watched with pride as she exchanged her vows in the traditional *nikah* ceremony. It's tradition for the father of the bride to give his daughter away, and as the imam made the official declaration and I said good-bye to Arooj, I wished her the best. I always thought that seeing the newlyweds leaving the mosque that day would be the lasting image I'd have of our house of worship.

Never could I have imagined that, almost fifteen years later, I would be weeping and praying across the street while our mosque was engulfed in flames.

My family and I moved to Victoria in 1984. I had three young children then and a small medical practice. We decided to relocate to Victoria because we thought it was a better area to raise our children. We were just the second Muslim family to settle in Victoria at that time. For the next few years, there were only a handful of Muslims living in town. We would sometimes pray together on Fridays and take turns hosting.

Our community began to grow at the turn of the decade. Several new Muslim families moved to town, and there were a few Muslim-owned businesses too. We came together regularly for prayers and meals. This encouraged more Muslims to settle in Victoria. A local Muslim physician then gifted us a house, and we had our daily prayers there.

A lot of Muslim families have come and gone from the city. Victoria's population is roughly seventy thousand, and like many midsize cities in America, we have several factories and plants. Many Muslim engineers and workers rotated in and out of them. It's wonderful when new members join the community and sad when they say good-bye.

We nevertheless continued to grow. Today there are forty to forty-five Muslim families in town, roughly 160 to 170 community members in total. We are a diverse community. We are engineers, primary caregivers, business people, and physicians, and we represent more than a dozen nationalities. My wife and I are from Pakistan.

Ours is the only Muslim family that has been here since the 1980s. We raised our children in Victoria, and they graduated from high school and college here. Arooj recently moved back to Victoria with her husband. We're so happy she came home.

The Islamic Center of Victoria had its grand opening in May 2000. Thirty Muslim families lived in town then, and they all attended the celebration. It was a beautiful sunny day. The grand opening was open to the public and hundreds of local community members joined us. Even the media came.

We were joined by numerous distinguished guests. Yusuf Islam, the singer formerly known as Cat Stevens, attended and spoke about his conversion to Islam. Hakeem "The Dream" Olajuwon, the former center for the Houston Rockets and an NBA Hall of Fame inductee, attended as well. The children were thrilled to meet him! He was one of the biggest celebrities in Texas. He's also a devout Muslim.

Our community felt safe and welcome in Victoria. We mingled with everyone. Not even the events of 9/11 changed that. Despite the terrible shock, on the day after 9/11 the local interfaith community, police, town officials, and mayor gathered in front of the mosque and proclaimed unity and support for our Muslim community. We didn't ask for this gesture of support; they offered it. It meant the world to us because the mosque was only one year old and we didn't know what to expect. We came together as one community.

It was business as usual for many years after that. We lived in peace and solidarity with the broader Victoria community. We contributed to fundraisers and charitable organizations. We participated in social and interfaith activities. We delivered presentations on Islam at other houses of worship. Local churches and schools sent their students to the mosque to learn about our religious traditions. The mosque became a community center. Our children played there, and we held potluck dinners there every Friday. Non-Muslims and interfaith friends sometimes joined.

Then, in 2015, a few teenagers painted some graffiti on the front of the mosque. We couldn't decipher the writing. A local newspaper read it as "H8," or shorthand for "hate." There was a positive outcome, though. The boys who committed the vandalism confessed to their parents, the parents brought their children to the mosque, and the boys apologized to our congregation. They were teenagers who attended one of the local high schools. The community quickly forgave them and welcomed the boys into our community. They later joined us for prayer, and their families came to a potluck dinner at the mosque.

Although we opposed prosecution, the district attorney's office brought criminal charges, and the boys were given community service. They helped us with yard work at the mosque one weekend and completed their service.

We opposed prosecution because we thought it would increase animosity and misunderstanding. The children had accepted responsibility, looked us in the eye, and apologized. We had reached an acceptable resolution based on forgiveness and reconciliation. Forgiveness is fundamental to our faith. In that moment, we weren't just reflecting our beliefs. We were reflecting the practices and traditions of Islam.

The most basic tenet of Islam is to be a true believer and obey the commands of God, the one and only god who created the universe. We are all created equal before God, and we must be respectful and live in service to others. Do unto others as you would have them do unto you. We also believe that we are responsible for our deeds. We will all be resurrected one day to stand before God and account for our time in this world. If we worship only him, and live responsibly and faithfully alongside our family, community, and country, then we will be blessed and go to heaven.

As a devout Muslim, I have conservative values and generally lean Republican. But the 2016 Presidential election was different. I couldn't support Donald Trump for president of the United States. The values he advocated, including discrimination on the basis of faith, ethnicity, and national origin, aren't conservative values.

Many say that mullahs and other religious leaders exploit Islam and create terrorists. I don't think a leader alone can make a person do something. But a leader can exploit a person's inner fears and beliefs and make it more likely for that person to act on those fears and beliefs. Many terrorists today, for example, harbor ill will against the West, sentiments that religious leaders often channel and abuse.

Trump is no different. He exploited widespread misunderstanding and fear of Muslims. When Trump said he would ban Muslims or require them to register, he cultivated this inner fear. Just as there are mullahs who capitalize on bitterness towards non-Muslims, Trump channeled and exploited anti-Muslim sentiment. That's in part why Islamophobia and incidents of anti-Muslim hate have spiked since his campaign and election. Those who felt inhibited were empowered to act out.

Much of this hate originates with the media. The majority of the 1.8 billion Muslims in this world are peace-loving, true followers of Islam. Only a tiny fraction of so-called Muslims support terrorism. Our faith unequivocally condemns terrorism. But if you listen to the media, you would think that most Muslims are terrorists, and that only Muslims are capable of terrorist acts. Our entire faith is put on trial every time a Muslim commits a terrible act of violence. No other community bears this burden.

Still, life in Victoria remained the same during the campaign and election. We didn't encounter any animosity. That soon changed, though. In mid-January of this year, the mosque was burglarized. One morning, we saw that the back door had been broken into. As we walked through the facility, we noticed that several computers and phones were missing. We called the police, and they boarded the doors and launched an investigation.

Then, just one week later, my phone rang in the middle of the night. It was the imam of the mosque. He was frantic and said, "The mosque is on fire!" He was in shock.

I jumped out of bed and started running. I didn't even wake up my wife. I just ran. As I drove on the highway and approached the mosque, I could see the smoke coming from the top of the building.

When I saw the mosque in flames, I cried. I watched from across the street as the fire fighters worked hard to put out the fire. The gas station at the corner of the street had spotted it first and called 911.

We alerted our families and the community. Some of them came right away. There were fifteen to twenty of us, and we stood there in the middle of the night watching the mosque burn to the ground. Many of us were in our nightclothes. Then it began to rain. At 5 a.m., we performed morning prayer in the rain, watching our house of worship burn.

We wouldn't be able to get onto the mosque grounds for another three days. The police had to cordon it off, investigate the fire, and collect evidence. Later that morning, the entire community came to my house. There were dozens of people there, including friends from the neighboring city of Corpus Christi. We were heartbroken. Many of us were inconsolable because the pain and shock were so great. I get emotional talking about it even today. We sat, cried, and decided how to move forward.

We agreed to hold a prayer service across the street from the mosque the following day. It would be open to the public. More than four hundred people joined us that Sunday. The police closed the street on both sides. I remember it vividly. People poured in from every direction. Interfaith leaders spoke.

Community members spoke. Friends from Dallas, Houston, and Corpus Christi joined as well.

In the subsequent days, weeks, and months, there was an outpouring of support from the local Victoria community and the world. We heard from former community members, friends, elected officials, and Muslim leaders. Churches and synagogues offered us a place to worship. We received hundreds of messages and cards. Schoolchildren hand drew notes for us; church members knitted for us. A GoFundMe campaign raised $1.1 million in funds for mosque reconstruction. We received donations from over ninety countries. I still have patients who come in, hug me, and offer their condolences. Some even come with a check, even though we're no longer collecting donations.

But it was still a very difficult time for the community. The conversations with our children were tough. Many of them had grown up at the mosque. They had played there when they were little. They had learned about the Islamic faith there, and celebrated holidays and birthdays there. It was the only mosque some of them had ever known. Nothing could bring back those cherished memories.

We told our younger ones that we lost our prayer space, but didn't show them the shocking photos. Our imam used his religious teachings to counsel them, and we had a psychologist sit down with them, too. Even Arooj was devastated. She got married in that mosque. A part of her history had been lost forever. But we had to remain strong because the children were watching. We want them to always love their faith.

Today we use a portable building that was previously used for school activities as our community center. That building is adjacent to the mosque and escaped the fire. We cleaned it up, decorated it, laid out carpets, and made it our new home. This is where we pray and meet. The mosque is in the process of being rebuilt, but full reconstruction will take several years.

Our community remains fearful. Many worry that we could be targeted again, especially living in Texas, where guns are so commonplace. After the hate crime, the community decided to hire a private security firm to guard our makeshift community center. They are on guard outside whenever we gather or the children play inside. It's sad that we need security to feel safe and that we worry about the safety of our little ones.

In June, federal prosecutors filed hate crime charges against the same man recently arrested for burglarizing the mosque in early January. In this case, we favored prosecution because of the gravity of the crime and his lack of remorse. We also thought hate crime charges were appropriate. He didn't target a random commercial building. He targeted a mosque. The law and prosecution must reflect that. While his arrest comforted some in the community, others still believe we have to be vigilant. If it happened before, why can't it happen again?

I don't know why this man targeted our community when he did. Was the attack brewing in his mind for a long time? Was his hatred long-standing and emboldened by the political climate and Trump? It's true that he set fire to the mosque just days after President Trump was inaugurated and the very same day that President Trump signed the first version of the Muslim ban. But I don't think he could have hatched his plan in just a few hours.

I do know, though, that he hated Islam. He hated Muslims. He burglarized our mosque. He set it on fire. He terrorized our community. We later learned from the police that he expressed hate against Muslims on Facebook and that he believed mosque members were colluding with ISIS and maybe stockpiling weapons. It's always the same story, and one that Trump keeps promoting. People think innocent, peace-loving Muslims are terrorists. Islamophobia is real, and it's growing, and it struck our peace-loving community in Victoria.

We must all work to combat misunderstanding and hate. Muslims must continue to educate the world about their faith and lead honorable lives. We must show the world that we live in love and harmony with different communities worldwide.

Non-Muslims must be willing to listen to us and challenge

their inner fears. They should invite their Muslim neighbors to their houses of worship to explain their faith. They must be mindful of the media as well and differentiate fact from fiction. Just as Muslims have a duty to educate the world about our traditions, non-Muslims have a reciprocal duty to understand the real teachings of Islam before casting judgment.

We've done that work in Victoria for decades, and will do it for as long as we can.

8

TANYA GERSH

Tanya Gersh is a Jewish American real estate agent and wedding planner who lives in Whitefish, Montana.

ON THE FIRST SATURDAY OF 2017, I WOKE UP EARLY, ATE BREAKfast, and got dressed. The temperature was below zero, and I put on some of my warmest clothes. I wore big sunglasses, a large scarf, and a hat. I didn't want to be recognized.

I was about to attend a rally in Whitefish, Montana, and didn't know what to expect. In more than twenty years in Whitefish, I couldn't recall a single protest in our small town. And yet I was ready to join the "Love Not Hate" rally, a public stand against oppression and anti-Semitism. A neo-Nazi march was scheduled to take place just nine days later and its ending point was my home. I was one of the targets.

When I arrived, I didn't see the one hundred people that many had expected, I saw more than five hundred warmly bundled souls gathered in minus-seven-degree weather, holding signs and placards with messages of peace and solidarity. I saw an area for children, a warming station with hot drinks, and a section for food donations. I saw media asking questions, taking interviews, and filming speeches and performances on stage. Local officials, musicians, artists, and interfaith leaders all preached a similar message that day: Love trumps hate.

I wanted to embrace everyone there. I couldn't believe it. They were there for me.

I come from humble beginnings. Neither of my parents was educated and both took whatever jobs they could find. I got my first job at the age of fourteen. I've always been a small-town mountain girl. I grew up in Idaho and paid my way through college. I chose the University of Montana because I was eligible for in-state tuition under the Western Undergraduate Exchange program. It was one of the most affordable schools in the region. I met my husband in Montana, and we later moved to Whitefish. That was more than twenty years ago.

My faith has always been very important to me. Both my parents and grandparents were Jewish, and I knew that I wanted to marry a Jewish man and raise Jewish children. My connection to the faith was unconventional, though, because I never lived in a city with a large Jewish population or synagogue. The community was usually small and functioned more like a club or organization than a congregation. We met in local churches or community centers, just like we do in Whitefish.

I've learned so much about Judaism by virtue of having lived in small Jewish communities. I learned to lead services because rabbis often didn't live in my town. Community members would get together to study Torah, learning from one another. There are about thirty Jewish families in Whitefish today. We get together once a month and on every major holiday.

Prior to recent events, I had never experienced anti-Semitism or bigotry. Maybe I've led a sheltered life. But I've generally felt welcome and accepted. My neighbors have always been eager to learn about my faith, and the schools in Whitefish regularly invited my husband and me to discuss our religious traditions on Jewish holidays.

As soon as we moved to Whitefish, we jumped right into the community. I started a bridal business and became the go-to person for events and local happenings. My business blossomed. I had a six-page spread in *Brides* magazine and built a national reputation for planning country-chic weddings. My clientele spanned the nation.

My husband, Judah, started a law practice. He provided all kinds of services, including real estate advice. He worked hard, and the community trusted him. Seeing his success and wanting a change, I later became a real estate agent. Plus, we started a family, and I wanted to spend time with our two boys.

We loved our small community. We cherished the mountain air, clean water, and healthy living. The city sits on the outskirts of Glacier National Park, and there are wildlife and mountains everywhere you turn. It's a peaceful and beautiful way of life. There's nowhere in the world I'd rather raise our two boys. They're now ten and thirteen.

When Trump announced his candidacy and hit the trail, life in Whitefish didn't change much. Whitefish is one of the only towns in Montana that leans Democrat; the rest of the state leans Republican. In 2016, Whitefish voted for Clinton; the rest of the state voted for Trump. Our community was shocked by the result, but didn't think it would impact us.

We were wrong. In late November, Richard Spencer, an extremist alt-right leader, raised his glass at a conference in Washington, DC, and shouted, "Hail Trump! Hail our people! Hail victory!"[1] The clip went viral, and many of his followers parroted him with Nazi salutes. That single line and salute changed our lives and the town of Whitefish forever.

Spencer believes that whites are a superior race and wants to purge the U.S. of all communities of color and minorities. Spencer lives part-time in Whitefish, a fact he loves to share with his followers. His mother, Sherry Spencer, has a home and a commercial building in town.

When word spread about the salute, the whole town started talking. Some were angry; others were scared. Would hateful people move to our city? Would we lose the tranquility and love that we so cherish? Would we lose tourism, the bread and butter of our local economy? There was talk of a protest outside the commercial building that Sherry Spencer owned. I personally witnessed people stopping and taking pictures of the building, and was worried about the safety and businesses of the tenants. Some of them were my friends. So I called the tenants and recommended that they put a sticker or statement of love in their windows in order to show that they did not support Richard Spencer's ideologies.

I later received a call from Sherry. She asked me, "Tanya, what would you do?" I told her if it were my son, I would sell the building, donate some of the profits to a human rights cause, and state publicly that I didn't believe in my son's ideology. It was a peaceful and heartfelt conversation, and we spoke mother-to-mother. I offered to help with the sale, and she seemed genuinely interested. But she later changed her mind and told me she wanted to pursue other avenues. I wished her the very best, and we left it at that.

Several days later, Sherry published an article on the blog site *Medium*, accusing me of trying to extort her. I was shocked. I never tried to extort her; I tried to help her. But my opinion and the truth didn't matter. Neo-Nazis and white supremacists jumped to her defense and put a target on my back.

The day after the *Medium* post, the Daily Stormer, one of the most popular alt-right extremist websites in the country, published an article entitled "Jews Targeting Richard Spencer's Mother for Harassment and Extortion—TAKE ACTION!" Andrew Anglin, the publisher of the blog and an apparent friend of Richard Spencer, urged his thousands of followers to launch a "troll storm" against my family. This was the same man who wrote after the election, "Our Glorious Leader has ascended to God Emperor. Make no mistake about it: we did this. If it were not for us, it wouldn't have been possible."[2]

His agenda was clear. He wanted to intimidate, harass, and terrorize my family. The post included photographs of my family and our contact information, including phone numbers, email addresses, and links to our social media profiles. It even had my older son's Twitter handle. They also photoshopped an image of me to include a yellow Star of David, just like the ones Jews were required to wear during World War II. "Just make your opinions known. Tell them you are sickened by their Jew agenda," he wrote. "And hey–if you're in the area, maybe you should stop by and tell her in person what you think of her actions."[3]

Those first few days are blurry because I really feared for my life, as did my entire family. I remember arriving home the evening that the Daily Stormer published the post and seeing Judah sitting quietly in our bedroom. Suitcases were sprawled across the floor, and he told me that I had to pack my belongings. As he showed me the article on the computer in the dim light, I froze. I had never heard of a troll storm or the Daily Stormer. Why did they hate Jews? Would they show up at my home? Would they hurt my children? We didn't know whether to leave or to stay. We locked the doors, closed the binds, and wept. I've never seen Judah cry like that.

Then the phone calls started. The first few were of gunshots. To this day, gunshots and other loud noises terrify me. That was just the beginning. Over the next many months, I received more than seven hundred hateful anti-Semitic telephone calls, voicemails, texts, emails, social media messages, letters, and postcards of hate. The hate came in every form, at every time of day. They threatened me. They threatened my husband. They threatened our friends. Even my children weren't spared. The

references to extermination, ovens, and Auschwitz were endless.
My lawyers and I publicly released some of the messages. They
included:

> Thanks for demonstrating why your race needs to be collectively
> ovened.

> You have no idea what you are doing, six million are only the
> beginning.

> We are going to keep track of you for the rest of your life.

> You will be driven to the brink of suicide. We will be there to take
> pleasure in your pain and eventual end.

> You really should have died in the Holocaust with the rest of your
> people.

The Daily Stormer, meanwhile, continued to mobilize its
online army. They published additional articles about me and
photoshopped an image of my older son and me at the entrance
gate to the Auschwitz concentration camp. Anglin called for an
armed march on Martin Luther King Day, and promised that
they would march through town to protest "Jews" and "Jewish
businesses." The march would end at my home. The flier adver-
tising the march featured my photo; another flier featured an
image of my head being speared.

We ultimately stayed in Whitefish because we didn't want to
run. But we barely left our home the first few weeks. We locked
the doors and closed the shades. We consulted the police and
took security measures that I'm not at liberty to share. The local
police constantly patrolled our neighborhood, and we were in
close contact with the FBI. We were in a suspended state of shock.

The conversations with our children were really hard. I talked to them about anti-Semitism and the Holocaust. All Jewish
parents struggle with when to have this conversation with their
children. I didn't have a choice. They had to know their history.
All of it. My ten-year-old son missed thirty days throughout the
school year, and some of his teachers sent notes homes saying
they were worried about him. He cried a lot. So did I.

•

The only reason I survived those few weeks and all that ensued was my community. From the moment I was attacked, they stood tall. The community set up a "love drive" and dropped off letters, cards, gifts, flowers, and baskets. People across the country and world supported us, too. They sent cookies and chocolates with messages like "Stay strong" and "We stand with you." There was an outpouring of love from Jewish classrooms, Christian church groups, and day schools. A Muslim knitting group sent letters and called my children "heroes."

A local advocacy group based here in Whitefish, Love Lives Here, also sprang into action and mobilized people in support of inclusivity and tolerance. In January, they organized the "Love Not Hate" rally, which drew more than five hundred people out in the frigid cold. Many local businesses joined the effort as well and put "Love Not Hate" stickers or menorahs in their windows. The Daily Stormer later published a list of these businesses and asked their readers to target them. These businesses were threatened and received bad reviews online. But none of them caved. They persevered and continued to stand by my side.

The community stood so strong that the armed march scheduled for Martin Luther King Day never happened. Nobody showed up. Instead, the community held a gathering of peace that afternoon during which they served a Jewish favorite, matzoh ball soup, to the entire community. Later that evening, the community held a concert, and a famous local musician and former political candidate, Rob Quist, dedicated a song to me, "Love Song for Tanya." My family and I were overcome with emotion as we huddled around the laptop and watched the concert live on Facebook. We had left town because we were still worried that the march would take place and that we might be targeted.

Still, the hate I endured forever changed my life. I'm a different person today than I was before. I used to live my life through rose-colored glasses. I was a glass-full kind of person. I saw the best in everything and the beauty in everyone. I was the person who'd become best friends with a stranger at a restaurant. I no longer have that positive energy and optimistic spirit. I don't trust strangers. I don't assume people have my best interest at heart.

I see a psychiatrist regularly and was recently diagnosed with a classic case of post-traumatic stress disorder. I struggle with anxiety and get scared often. If somebody is walking really fast in my direction, I get anxious. If a car makes a quick U-turn, my heart races. I cry often, have nightmares, and struggle to get a good night's rest. I don't like my picture being taken. I still receive hateful messages today and worry that someone may target my family.

I worked really hard to build my business and my digital footprint. If you googled me before this happened, you would have seen my website and a portfolio of my work: photos of weddings I planned, and properties I sold. If you google my name today, the first search result that comes up is "filthy jew." If you scroll further down, you see my name and photo on a website dedicated to "homewreckers." You see stories and images threatening violence against me. I am working to rebuild my businesses. In the beginning, I was terrified to take on new listings and expose my clients to potential harassment. So much of my success was built online and spread by word of mouth. Strangers destroyed decades of hard work.

Being targeted on account of my faith was particularly hard for me. You can't take the Jewish out of me. It's my heritage. It's my blood. It's my soul. Looking back today, this experience brought me closer to my people. I've always referred to the Jewish people who escaped the war or died in the Holocaust as my family. Now I truly feel that.

I also feel a closeness to other minority communities. I'm not an activist. But I've been thinking a lot about the mothers of black, Latinx, Muslim, and queer children, and all they've done to keep their children safe. They've become my family, too. I know that the pain I've experienced is measured in months, and theirs is measured in generations. But I still feel a connection to them, knowing what they've endured and how they've struggled. My heart breaks for them.

I'm fighting back by bringing a lawsuit against Andrew Anglin, the publisher of the Daily Stormer. I'm really grateful to the Southern Poverty Law Center for representing me. In fact, it was SPLC that first helped us to understand the white supremacist movement, the Daily Stormer, and their extremist tactics. The police didn't know what to do because they had limited experience responding to trolls and this form of abuse. We filed suit in Montana federal court, claiming invasion of privacy, intentional infliction of emotional distress, and harassment and intimidation. I truly believe that what they did to me isn't protected by free speech. They targeted me, and that's against the law.

Nothing would have hurt me more than giving up. Being a victim is painful. But surviving and fighting back has brought me a sense of peace and justice. As long I'm alive, I want to fight and make sure that nobody else endures this again. Plus, I love the idea of a Jewish family in Whitefish, Montana, fighting the biggest neo-Nazi in America!

I remember telling my children when Trump was first elected president that there would be no Trump jokes in our home. That he was our president, whether we voted for him or not, and we needed to try to be respectful.

When asked about President Trump in some of the early interviews after the incident, I was respectful and said, "No comment." What did he have to do with what happened to me? Even when he was slow to respond to the desecration of synagogues and mosques, I gave him the benefit of the doubt. Terrible things happen in our country every day. But Charlottesville changed everything.

When I watched the television coverage of the white supremacist march in Charlottesville and saw torch-wielding extremists yelling "Jews will not replace us" and "Blood and Soil," I saw in their eyes the same people who were terrorizing my family, who called, messaged, and emailed us. This was them in living, breathing form.

I can't forgive our president for suggesting that there was a moral equivalence between white supremacists and protesters. That was a moral failure. I now encourage my children to have open and critical conversations in our home because it's clear that this president doesn't have our back.

I was thrilled with the response of major technology companies after the events of Charlottesville. GoDaddy and Google refused to host the web domain of the Daily Stormer. Twitter and Facebook removed users who spewed hate. Uber and Airbnb decided that they wouldn't let hateful extremists use their platforms.

The truth is that it should have happened a long time ago. These companies have a responsibility to curb hate. Why should hateful people be allowed to use their services to spread hate? The neo-Nazis took my life away, but the internet helped them do it.

What gives me hope is the activists who fight every day to make this world a better place—people from all walks of life standing up for Jews, Muslims, communities of color, and other vulnerable groups. I believe that most of the world is on the right side and wants change. It's our diversity that distinguishes us and makes us beautiful. I will forever teach this to my children. I don't want them to be afraid. I don't want them to be afraid of being Jewish. I want them to know that there will always be people who stand up for love and justice, just like Heather Heyer did. I didn't know Heather, but I think about her all the time. When she took a stand, she stood up for me. She stood up for all of us. She's my hero.

9

HARJIT KAUR

The U.S. Department of Health and Human Services defines bullying as "unwanted, aggressive behavior among school aged children that involves a real or perceived power imbalance. The behavior is repeated, or has the potential to be repeated, over time. . . . Bullying includes actions such as making threats, spreading rumors, attacking someone physically or verbally, and excluding someone from a group on purpose."[1]

In early 2016, Harjit Kaur, a longtime Sikh activist and civil rights lawyer based in San Jose, California, learned that her nephew, Akal, was being bullied in school.

ONE AFTERNOON IN THE SPRING OF 2016, I RECEIVED A CALL from my thirteen-year-old nephew, Akal. He asked me if immigrants are bad people. I asked him why he said that, and he told me he was being called an "immigrant boy" in class. He said students told him to go home and called him a terrorist. They'd hit and shove him. One student yelled at him, "Trump will become president and get rid of terrorists and send them home." Akal felt scared, unwanted, and un-American. He was born and raised in California. America is the only home he has ever known.

Akal would come home from school and cry. What pained him most was that nobody would stand up for him. Many students remained silent or looked the other way, even those he considered friends.

Akal is a devout Sikh boy, and grows his hair long. Sikh boys tie their hair in a topknot which they cover with a square piece of cloth called a *patka*.

Sikhism was founded in 1469. It challenged prevailing systems of social and religious inequality, including India's caste system. Devotion to one god, truthful living, and selfless service are the basic tenets of the faith. Sikhism has since grown to be the fifth largest religion in the world. There are over 500,000 Sikhs in the United States, with the largest populations found in California and on the East Coast. Devout Sikhs are identifiable by their distinct items of dress and appearance: *kesh* (unshorn hair), *kanga* (small wooden comb), *kara* (iron bracelet), *kirpan* (religious article resembling a knife), and *kachera* (shorts, as a reminder of chastity). Many adult Sikhs cover their hair with a turban, a symbol of pride and equality.

The impact of the bullying on Akal was immediate and heartbreaking. In addition to the insults and physical assaults he suffered, he had trouble making friends, and his peers refused to partner with him on group assignments. The teachers didn't know what was happening, and would ask Akal why he didn't have any partners. The bullying was particularly bad during recess because of the lack of supervision. Akal felt isolated and alone.

His grades and self-esteem suffered. He lost interest in school and extracurricular activities. He sometimes got into trouble with teachers and administrators. It was often his version of the story against others'. Akal was usually blamed. This is symptomatic of what happens to bullied students. There's an assumption that they're part of the problem.

Akal's experience is similar to that of many diverse youth, including Muslim, Arab, LGBTQIA, immigrant, and black students. Studies show that more than 50 percent of Sikh and Muslim students are bullied in school on account of their religious identity. In some cases, youth are bullied for multiple characteristics or traits, including their accent, faith, national origin, and race. Cyberbullying is particularly widespread in today's world, as the internet is available long after children leave the classroom.

Akal's parents didn't know what to do. They were immigrants from Punjab, India, home to roughly half of the Sikh population in the world, and they had no idea how to stop the bullying. English is their second language.

We were really worried. Students who are bullied are more likely to experience depression, anxiety, sadness, loneliness, and isolation. They may also experience changes in sleeping and eating patterns and health habits. Many students who are bullied experience a decline in their academic achievement and are more likely to miss school or drop out altogether, as well.

His teacher tried to help by punishing the bullies and separating them from Akal, but that didn't work. Akal and his parents asked me to intervene. I became the advocate for the family. I mediated between Akal and the school, and helped develop a plan that would end the bullying. As a civil rights activist, attorney, and anti-bullying advocate, I've helped many students, parents, and schools respond to bullying.

The first thing I did was offer emotional support to Akal to help him regain his confidence. I told him he belonged in that class. I told him he should be proud to be an immigrant. I told him about the many contributions that immigrants had made to the state of California and the U.S., including Sikh Americans. I recounted the story of Dalip Singh Saund, the first Sikh congressman, who held office from 1957 to 1963 in the 29th Congressional District of California. I reminded him that Sikh history was recently added to California's History and Social Sciences Curriculum. That made Akal really proud. Between 2015 and 2016, Akal worked on that campaign and obtained petition signatures in support of including Sikh history in California textbooks.

Next, we discussed how to stop the bullying. Akal didn't want to punish his classmates, because he thought it would aggravate them further. Instead, he wanted to reach out to his peers, educate them, and be treated as an equal.

I agreed with Akal. Forgiveness and reconciliation are core beliefs of the Sikh faith. Studies also show that zero tolerance anti-bullying policies do not work. Suspension, expulsion, and other significant forms of punishment intensify aggression in the classroom. Also, kids who exhibit bullying behavior need help, too. They are more likely to abuse alcohol and drugs as adolescents and adults. They are also more likely to get into fights, engage in criminal activity, and be abusive towards others.

I gave multiple Sikh-awareness presentations in Akal's class over the next few weeks. I discussed the history of the faith, our identity, and why Akal covered his hair. I also met with school officials and discussed the best way to prevent, identify, and curb bullying. These kinds of presentations and meetings are commonplace for Sikh parents and close kin. When our children are bullied, we have few options other than to spring into action.

In Akal's case, the intervention seemed to work. Students approached Akal, asked him about his faith, and invited him to join their group of friends. The bullying started to subside, and he was beginning to feel like any other student.

But there were others who continued to bully Akal. Some of them had obtained notes from their parents excusing them from my presentations on the grounds of religious freedom.

This is a huge issue in schools. Some parents refuse to let their children learn about other faiths because they believe that schools are religion-free zones. I think this is absurd. Students should learn about all faiths in school. Excusing students from interfaith presentations encourages hostility and bullying in the classroom and promotes the idea of "other." No child wants to be labeled as an "other" in school, as it perpetuates social isolation.

Akal's sixth-grade classroom mirrors so much of America. Sometimes our divisions seem irreconcilable.

I believe the political climate is to blame. In the last few years, especially in recent months, community reports of bullying have spiked nationwide. I've received dozens of calls from Sikh parents asking me to help their children. Trump's rhetoric, policies, and political appointments have bred discrimination and racism nationwide, especially against immigrants and those perceived to be Muslim. I believe that the bullying that Akal recently endured was the direct result of Trump's rhetoric on the campaign trail.

Roughly two weeks after our intervention, the bullying stopped. Akal began to feel more comfortable at school, and was engaging with his peers. I asked a friend to tutor Akal after school to rebuild his confidence and interest in his studies. This gave him an opportunity to create positive associations with learning and to have another positive role model. Akal also healed by writing daily in a journal, a practice he continues today. Nevertheless, Akal sometimes has trouble talking about what he endured. The very act of recounting his experience can re-traumatize him.

As a domestic violence survivor myself and an activist, I'm very sensitive to the trauma that bullying and abuse can cause. There is no one-size-fits-all solution. The approach must be multifaceted and include conversations with students and their families, the school, and, in some cases, community representatives. That's especially true right now, when entire communities are under threat. The needs of the child must be the driving consideration.

Schools likewise need to implement policies and procedures that foster a safe and healthy learning environment. Teachers and administrators should receive regular training on how to combat bullying. Diversity training is also important because school officials often aren't aware of the cultural richness in their own classroom. In fact, sometimes teachers do the bullying. Language is important, too. Labeling a student a bully or victim can be dangerous, because students often take on that identity. Negative associations with terms like bully and victim can endure for a long time.

Akal showed great strength and humility throughout the ordeal. He stood up for himself, sought my help, and even forgave. He is now in middle school and has many friends. We have discussed the very real possibility that he may encounter bullying again, but he continues to draw courage and inspiration from his faith. He recently graduated sixth grade with honors from the President's Education Awards Program. He received a certificate signed by President Trump, the irony of which is not lost on Akal.

Akal's struggle isn't unique. Despite having settled in the U.S. more than a hundred years ago, Sikhs continue to experience many challenges in this county, including language access, employment discrimination, bigotry, and hate violence. Hate violence in particular terrorizes our communities. Our articles of faith make us easy targets, as Akal discovered.

In the days following 9/11, Balbir Singh Sodhi was murdered in a hate crime in Mesa, Arizona. This was the first of several documented hate crimes that were reported as probable acts of retaliation for the 9/11 terrorist attacks. The murderer reportedly told friends that he was "going to go out and shoot some towel-heads."[2]

On March 4, 2011, two Sikh grandfathers, Gurmej Singh Atwal and Surinder Singh, were murdered in Elk Grove,

California. And on August 5, 2012, a gunman shot and killed six Sikhs and wounded several others at their house of worship, a *gurdwara*, in Oak Creek, Wisconsin. This domestic act of terrorism was one of the deadliest acts of violence against an American house of worship in our nation's history.

Yet today feels worse than 9/11 because our leaders are contributing so openly to this spike in hate. The president and his team have perpetuated the notion that immigrants, Muslims, and others are inherently dangerous.

And the hate crimes continue.

On September 25, 2016, Maan Singh Khalsa suffered severe physical and emotional trauma after he was attacked by three men at a Richmond, California, intersection. He was stabbed in the hand so deeply that his finger needed to be amputated, and his eye was swollen shut from being beaten. His attackers pulled off his turban and cut his hair, attacking his very identity as a Sikh. At the sentencing hearing for his attackers, Mr. Khalsa testified, "It will take many years, maybe the rest of my life, to heal from this attack. Just recognizing it as a hate crime is the first step in healing."

In March 2017, a Sikh man in Kent, Washington, was shot in the arm in his driveway by a masked gunman after being told to get out of the country. Luckily, he survived.

Sikhs continue to brave these challenges with humility and courage. In some cases, we're targeted because we're perceived to be Muslim, but we always reject the "mistaken identity" defense. Instead we stand shoulder to shoulder with our Muslim brothers and sisters and condemn all hate violence, no matter who it impacts. Dismissing the bigotry of today as a case of mistaken identity also diminishes our history and struggle.

Some community members believe our gurdwaras should have armed security and that we should carry guns. Others say that we shouldn't contribute to a culture of militarization and gun violence. These are issues that our gurdwaras will continue to discuss in the years ahead.

In the interim, Sikhs will continue to practice their faith fearlessly and hold their heads up high. It's what we call *Chardi Kala*, a mental state of optimism and courage. No matter what happens, we always maintain a spirit of ascending energy and positivity. It's a way of life. We've always faced struggle and risen above it, just like Akal.

10

DESTINEE MANGUM AND WALIA MOHAMED

On May 26, 2017, Destinee Mangum, 16, and Walia Mohamed, 17, were aboard a MAX Light Rail train in Portland, Oregon, when a known white supremacist, Jeremy Joseph Christian, fatally stabbed two people, Ricky John Best and Taliesin Myrddin Namkai-Meche, and injured a third, Micah David-Cole Fletcher. Christian had attempted to assault people at a white supremacist "March for Free Speech" rally one month prior to the incident, and he insulted and threw a bottle at a black passenger on another MAX train one day before the fatal stabbing. This is the first time Destinee and Walia have spoken together publicly about what happened that fateful day.

Destinee: We weren't even supposed to be on the train that day. We got lost. We were on the train in the afternoon, when Christian got on at Lloyd Center. It's a main stop in central Portland. For like eight minutes, he just yelled at us:

"You're nothing"; "Kill yourself"; "Get out of this country"; "Burn."

Walia: "Muslims should die." "Go back to Saudi Arabia." As soon as he got on the train, he started yelling at us. It's like our faces were a trigger. I felt like he was attacking me because I was wearing a hijab; Destinee was wearing something on her head, too. He was yelling stuff about Muslims and Christians as well. Plus, we're both black. He was racist and didn't like that either.

Destinee: While he yelled, he was staring right at us and holding some book. He had this look in his eyes like he really didn't care. His eyes were blank.

Walia: It was terrifying. And he was a big guy. We feared for our lives. I remember this African American guy standing right in front of us. He did nothing.

Destinee: Nothing.

Walia: I mean, he said in a low voice to Christian, "Could you calm down?" I wish he had done more. After Christian got louder and more aggressive, I got really scared. That's when we moved to the back of the train.

Destinee: I also remember that when Christian was yelling, there was another white guy vouching for him. He was standing right behind him and saying yes to everything Christian was saying.

Walia: He was agreeing with him, just nodding his head.

Destinee: Christian kept yelling at us, even when we were in the back. That's when Ricky, Taliesin, and Micah stepped in. They were all on the train together and spoke up.

Walia: They didn't even know each other. They just wanted to help. I don't remember what happened next.

Destinee: I saw a knife.

Walia: When he started stabbing, we ran as fast as we could. The train had already stopped, but it should have stopped earlier.

Destinee: The conductor should have stopped the train much earlier. This didn't happen in two seconds or even a few minutes. It took a long time for this to happen. Before Ricky, Taliesin, and Micah intervened, nobody said nothing. Nobody did anything. There's an emergency button. Nobody pushed it.

Walia: I still don't know why nobody pushed the emergency button. It's like people froze.

Destinee: When Christian ran off, we ran in the opposite direction. I called my mom. I panicked. I was crying. "Mom, Mom, Mom, Mom."

She said, "What's wrong? What's wrong? Calm down. Talk to me."

I told her, "Somebody got stabbed on the MAX. I don't know what's going on. Can you just come get me?"

My mom said, "I'm on my way."

Walia: She knew something terrible had happened.

Destinee: I'm grateful they intervened. I don't know how to feel because people lost their lives. It's almost like you didn't want them to step up. But if they didn't, where would I be?

Walia: You feel bad, but thankful. I feel thankful because they saved my life.

Destinee: We're in touch with Ricky's and Taliesin's families. It's been great meeting them and putting a face to the name. We recently met with Taliesin's sisters, and they showed us pictures of him at their family home. It was bittersweet. I felt so close to them.

Walia: It was sad for me. When I met them, all I could remember was the incident.

Destinee: I felt it was important to say thank you because I can't talk to those who passed away that day. Immediately after the incident, I messaged Ricky's, Taliesin's, and Micah's families, but nobody responded. I had to make sure they knew how I felt, and eventually they did. More media attention went to those who lost loved ones. That didn't make me feel bad. They did something out of this world, so, honestly, I'd pay them more attention, too.

Walia: They lost their lives, and we're still here, so I don't really care about that.

Destinee: I've always liked Portland, but it's uncomfortable now because I feel like everyone knows me. I don't know them, but they know me. A lot of people come up to me and say, "Oh my God. You're the girl from the MAX. Tell me about what happened."

Walia: It became a national story and it was too much for me. I didn't talk to anyone because I didn't like the attention. I hid because I didn't want the cameras on me. I had already been through so much. I just wanted my old life back. I also liked Portland growing up, but I don't feel comfortable here anymore. Everywhere I go, I fear for my safety. I'm a Somali immigrant and I decided to take off my hijab a few months ago because I don't feel safe. I feel like I'm going to get attacked again. Before the incident on the MAX, I had never been attacked. Not because of my hijab. Not for any reason. I'm still Muslim, but I just don't follow certain traditions because I feel unsafe. It's really hard for me right now.

Destinee: When I'm by myself, even at school, I'm always looking around wondering, *Who's that? What's on their mind? What are they thinking?* I can't focus in class. I'm looking over my shoulder all the time, 24-7, because I don't know what people are thinking or what they're going to do. Will they try to hurt me?

Walia: Ever since the incident, I feel like I have to be more careful. I worry when I go places because I don't like being around too many people. I feel anxious and like something's going to happen. It reminds me of that terrible day on the train. When I think about what happened, I feel like it was because of Trump. When we had Barack Obama as president, none of this was happening. They were not doing anything this extreme. But then Trump becomes president, and then everybody that was racist just comes out, like they're bold now. Since Trump is racist, they think it's okay to be racist. They're acting on their racist beliefs.

Destinee: It's getting out of hand. A lot has happened, even after Charlottesville, and Trump hasn't stepped up as president or said much. It shows that he doesn't care, or maybe that he supports them, in a way. Even when he finally said something about Portland, it wasn't much. He didn't say he cared. He didn't say he was in mourning. I remember. He basically let it slide. The Hispanics are being bullied in school and on social media. There are all these memes online about how Trump said they need to work on the border and build the wall. It's unfair and cruel. Also, I believe in Black Lives Matter, but there are other people in the world who are going through the same thing as black people. I feel like we should come together as one to help each other out. We're all being targeted because of our race or faith.

Walia: Latinos, immigrants, so many people. We're all going through the same thing.

Destinee: Our school was really supportive immediately after the incident. The security guards cried when they saw me. Every single teacher that saw me in the hallway said,

"Oh my God. I'm so sorry." They were very supportive. All my teachers. But at our new school, the reaction has been different. This school doesn't care. Nobody checks in on us. Not the counselors. Not the teachers. Nobody asks us if we're feeling comfortable. Nobody asks us if we need help or anything. We only have each other.

Walia: I just want someone to help me with college applications and university planning, but nobody cares at this new school.

Destinee: At this point, I don't really care about my story being told. This experience has showed me that a lot of people still don't care about me, even though they pretend like they do. They take advantage of me. I don't like going to benefit concerts, fundraisers, and stuff like that because every time it's been a let-down. Money is being raised for us, but we don't know where it's going. It's like a reality check.

Walia: They just want a story. Reporters and politicians want the attention. They care about the story so it can go viral and get lots of views and shares. Because when they get the story, they just leave. We don't hear from them again. It hurts.

Destinee: They violate our personal space. They show up at our door. For days and weeks after the incident, every time we came home, someone was looking for us. KPTV Fox 12, *Fox News*, *New York Times*, you name it. Everybody just came to our doorstep. They didn't talk to us beforehand. They didn't ask our permission. They just showed up. No respect. It was scary. You know them as television personalities, but you don't know them in real life. They could share my address with other people, and I don't even know how they got it in the first place. People contact us randomly even today.

The benefit concerts are meant to benefit them, not us.

The whole time, Walia and I walk through these places with random people and with nobody to protect us other than our family. We've asked for security before, but have never received it.

Walia: We need security.

Destinee: I've received calls and messages on Facebook and Instagram, saying things like, "I'm going to hunt you down and kill you. You don't deserve to be alive." Sometimes they call me "nigger." I just block them and try to forget about it. But what if they do come after me? A lot of people have been getting away with a lot of stuff. I told the police about the threats around the time of the grand jury, and they told me it would be okay. They said the aggressors were hiding behind screens and wouldn't do anything. After I insisted, they said they would watch my house, but I don't think they ever watched it. They said someone was going to drive by or check the perimeter a few times a day, but I didn't see anyone. I was threatened online just three weeks ago.

As of now, we've been quiet about everything. We haven't talked about it much, not even with each other. I feel like at some point Walia and I should talk about it more and go to therapy together. Post-traumatic stress disorder is real. I don't want to wait and be scarred for life. I also don't want that for Walia. I want us to do it together, not separately. We've tried to forget about it. But we can't forget about it. We're reminded of it every day.

Walia: We feel it. People remind us. Sometimes I just space out and think about it. It comes out of nowhere. It's everywhere.

Destinee: Or you see images. It's hard to ride past the scene. I haven't been back there since it happened. I don't even like passing the scene or seeing the MAX. I don't ride the train anymore.

Walia: I don't ride the train anymore, either.

Destinee: They gave their lives. Two people. We think about it 24-7.

Walia: I feel like it's never going to go away. It's always going to stay with us. No matter how old we get.

Destinee: No matter where we go. Walia's my sister and my best friend.

Walia: She'll always be my sister. No matter what. She's always going to be my family.

11

DOMINICK EVANS

A hateful climate can cause people to change their appearance or how they identify publicly. There is no way of knowing how many people have made this painful decision, nor to know the consequences on their lives.

Dominick Evans is a filmmaker/writer and a media advocate at the Center for Disability Rights.

I CAME OUT AS A TRANS MAN IN 2002, WHEN I WAS TWENTY-ONE. While I experienced microaggressions, discrimination, and hate because of it, rarely did I truly fear enough for my safety to hide who I was. That changed after the election and inauguration of Donald Trump. I now fear for my life and rarely publicly identify as trans.

We all know that white supremacists and neo-Nazis target racial and religious minorities, but they're often transphobic and homophobic, as well. I've been called a faggot, pervert, pedophile, and freak for more than a decade, but never with the intensity and hate I see today. White supremacists now act with impunity and think they have a license to hurt others. I fear that I could be next. I only leave my home for basic necessities and responsibilities. Other than shopping, medical appointments, and taking my son places, I feel like a prisoner in my own town.

Compounding this fear is the fact that I'm disabled. I've been in a wheelchair since I was sixteen years old.

I was born in Toledo, Ohio, and grew up just outside the city. I was born with a genetic neuromuscular disability, spinal muscular atrophy (SMA). It's a disability that affects the muscles and nerves, which affects movement and my ability to walk. I was diagnosed when I was four. For years, my mother was intent on forcing me to walk. She sent me to physical therapy when [it progressed to the point that] I could no longer walk, where I was forced to stand. I still remember feeling terrified because I couldn't move my legs. I thought I'd fall and hurt myself. This happens often with disabled people. Society focuses on a cure and making us "normal," rather than on our immediate needs, which in my case has been pain relief and accessibility.

My disability progressed as I got older, and when I was sixteen I started using a wheelchair full-time. It was such a relief. People see my wheelchair and feel sorry for me, but they don't realize that it gave me back my independence and mobility. It was a lifeline and made me less dependent on others. I'll be in a wheelchair for the rest of my life, and I am truly okay with that.

I had a very troubled childhood because I was bullied incessantly. When I was little, I had an awkward gait and would waddle when I walked. My peers would quack at me and call me "Duck." I had suicidal thoughts when I was five, and saw a therapist for years. The bullying continued into my high school years. People would exclude, ridicule, and even hit me. They would insult my family, often saying that my parents were horrible people and that my disability was God punishing them.

The worst incident happened when I was sixteen, just a week after I returned to school after missing five months due to surgery. I was using a scooter at the time. I had backed my scooter into the school elevator when a student frantically ran over and stopped me. He told me not to get into the elevator. I turned my scooter, and that's when I saw something, but I couldn't quite make out at first what it was. I was wearing a back brace at the time and couldn't really look down well. There were dead mice covering the floor of the elevator. Someone had put them there, hoping that I would run over them. I wept in school that day. It still makes me cry because it was the first time I was really scared. I feared for my life that day, just like I do today. Those responsible were never brought to justice, even though we had a good idea of who they were.

Being disabled is highly misunderstood in our society. My disability can cause respiratory complications, and I'm also asthmatic. I missed a lot of school, and my teachers weren't particularly empathetic. The only thing that kept me going was my grandparents. They helped raise me, and were often a source of encouragement and love.

I hated myself growing up. Sometimes I believed the awful things people said about me. What if I was not capable of anything? What if I was a freak nobody could love? I internalized messages from society proclaiming that I would die young and was half a person. These are things people with neuromuscular disabilities are often told. I didn't want to associate with other disabled folks because I didn't want to believe that I was disabled. I had internalized ableism—discrimination in favor of nondisabled people.

I only started identifying as disabled in college, after I befriended disabled activists. I will never forget the first time I saw so many disabled students whizzing across campus at Wright State University. I had never seen so many people using wheelchairs! They taught me about ableism, and I realized that my fears were unfounded. I'm not unlovable. I'm not going to die just because

I'm disabled. I'm not brave or courageous just by existing. I'm like any other person. I watch television, surf the internet, and listen to music. My disability doesn't solely define me. Once I stopped hating myself, the seeds of my activism were born.

Being comfortable with my disability also gave me the opportunity to explore my gender. When I was a child, I couldn't relate to my own body. It was as though I was disconnected from it. I thought I felt that way because of my disability, but after meeting other disabled folks, I realized it had nothing to do with that.

I started exploring and asking questions. I read about sexuality and gender, joined queer student groups on campus, and befriended queer students. The more I learned about the trans community, the more my life made sense. What others described, I felt. What they experienced, I understood. I had often felt more masculine than feminine growing up. I often identified with boys more than I did with girls. My body did not feel or look like I believed it should.

There wasn't a single moment when I realized I was trans. It was a process. But ever since I made the decision to publicly identify as trans and begin my transition, I've been a happier and more complete person. I feel more comfortable in my body. I'm free in a way that I wasn't before. I've since started taking hormones and had some surgery, and I've felt more like myself with each step forward in my transition.

I'm often asked why I'm this way. I don't know. Perhaps I was supposed to be born a male but was born a female. Maybe my brain was washed with testosterone in utero. Science will likely provide the answer one day. In the interim, I feel lucky to have been able to explore my gender. Disabled people are rarely seen as sexual or even gendered beings. We're often defined exclusively by our disability.

I identify as a nonbinary trans man rather than as a man because I don't want to wipe away my trans experience. Being perceived as a young girl/woman, I experienced terrible harassment and misogyny because of my gender. My life has been very different from cisgender men, and I cannot erase that. Those experiences inform much of my activism today.

When I think of the 2016 election, it pains me that the interests and needs of disabled people have been ignored. There are at least 58 million people in this country with some form of disability, including those in nursing homes, who don't get counted in the census. We're the world's largest minority, because we span every race, faith, sexual orientation, and gender. We're an important demographic, but are routinely disenfranchised because of ableism and limited political power.

The 2016 election was particularly hard on our community. Whenever vulnerable and disenfranchised communities are targeted, disabled people are impacted, too. We make for easy targets, especially those of us who use wheelchairs. What made 2016 worse was Trump's decision to openly mock a disabled person on the campaign trail—the reporter Serge Kovaleski. While that incident encouraged others to mock us, it also became a political talking point, which often excluded voices from the disability community.

Ever since the election, disabled folks have experienced an uptick in bullying and hate. I've seen it in my own life. People increasingly stare, ridicule, and follow me around. The microaggressions have spiked as well. In Trump's America, people are more rude and disrespectful, and less tolerant. They don't want to wait that extra minute for disabled folks to board a bus, cross the street, or go about our daily business. A close friend who's deaf was recently told to leave the country because he was using sign language in a public place. Some of us have had people stand over, or touch us, and recite a prayer asking God to heal us—something that happened occasionally before but seems more prevalent now.

The cybertrolling and online bullying have intensified as well. The online abuse is really distressing because disabled folks often rely on the internet for social interactions. We rely on social media to connect with one another, share our stories, and advocate for our rights, especially because the world remains largely inaccessible to many of us. Attacking and intimidating us online is hurtful and chilling. It makes us less likely to use one of the few outlets we have to connect.

The vitriolic debate over health care has intensified this discrimination and hate. This particularly hurts the disability community, as many of us rely on health care for independence and to stay alive. Health care is a civil and human right, and everyone should have equal and universal access to it. Unfortunately, communities of color, as well as people who are poor, elderly, and disabled, have often been deprived of such access. The Affordable Care Act, especially the Medicaid expansion, has helped remedy this inequity by making health care more affordable and accessible.

So, when politicians say we can't afford the ACA or it's unnecessary, what they're really saying is that our lives don't matter. Consider my disability. I need home- and community-based services (HCBS). I need help getting out of bed, getting in my wheelchair, going to the bathroom—things like that. This care allows me to live independently and pursue my dreams. Without this care, I would die or be forced into a nursing home, and they are often rife with abuse and neglect. In what can only be described as a state-sponsored form of hate, Trump and the GOP want to send us to our deaths. They also portray us as a tax liability on the American economy, rather than as contributing members of society. That fosters widespread bullying, discrimination, and hatred against many of us.

When disabled people speak out against this hate, we are often silenced or targeted. In early 2017, dozens of disabled activists descended onto Capitol Hill to protest proposed GOP healthcare legislation that would have significantly reduced access to HCBS. Protesters engaged in nonviolent civil disobedience and staged a die-in in Senator Mitch McConnell's office. Rather than meet with us, the GOP leadership attempted to block our access to their offices and later called the police, who then used excessive force on many of us. Some people were dragged out by their arms and legs, while others were dumped out of their wheelchairs. The images went viral.

I was a part of the media team for the national disability rights group ADAPT, which led these protests. We received some visibility that day, but we've been disappointed that the world has forgotten why we were there in the first place. In most of the coverage of the protests that followed, the media neglected to include the voices of the disabled activists who put their bodies on the line to save health care for everyone.

It's difficult enough being disabled in this political climate. Now I fear that people will learn that I'm trans as well. While Nazis have a long history of committing atrocities against disabled people, they put trans people at just as much risk. There are a number of white supremacist and neo-Nazi groups in Ohio, including in Cincinnati and Columbus, and their membership is growing. Some from Ohio joined the Charlottesville protests, yelling homophobic and transphobic slurs. I'm terrified that these same people who live in my town will target me if they learn I'm trans. Trans people, especially trans women of color, were targeted by hate before the election. It's even worse today.

In addition to homophobia and transphobia being on the rise, trans rights are also being rolled back. Just one month after taking office, the Trump administration revoked federal guidelines that allowed transgender students the right to use bathrooms and locker rooms that match their gender identity. Imagine trans girls being forced to use a bathroom with boys, or vice versa. That single decision jeopardizes the safety of countless trans students. We are also encountering increased discrimination at the state level, in what appears to be a trickle-down effect. From the time I was young, I've had HCBS because of my disability. Recently, though, I've had great difficulty getting this support because state officials are fixated on my gender. They've accused me of exaggerating my disability and denied me HCBS access because they say I'm "dressing up like a man."

There are times when I feel I should be more open and less afraid. There's nothing I'd rather do than be out all the time, but it's no longer safe. I have developed a strong instinct for self-preservation, and it tells me that things are different in Trump's America. I want to survive, even if that means hiding part of myself from others. I'm fortunate to have that option. Many people don't even realize that I'm trans. My disability often makes me appear genderless, as most people just see my wheelchair.

Those who are members of multiple disenfranchised communities are especially vulnerable right now. All of my black and brown disabled friends are afraid. All of my black and brown disabled trans friends are terrified. Friends have described being followed by white men in pickup trucks in cities across the country. In this sense, despite being both disabled and trans, I'm white and thus still privileged. I don't fear the police gunning me down or choking me to death. I don't fear people tying a noose around my neck. I may be a target of neo-Nazis, but I'm still a beneficiary of white privilege.

I worry about disabled and trans folks in America. We experience daily microaggressions, ridicule, and hate. We fear for our safety. We worry about health care. Sometimes, the frustration, hopelessness, and anger is all-consuming, and some in our community are pushed to suicide.

I've been able to press on because I'm part of a community of activists. I'm both a filmmaker/writer and a media advocate at the Center for Disability Rights. Disabled people are lawyers, doctors, scientists, and other professionals. So are trans folks. I'm committed to documenting our lives and stories through writing and film. We can't be reduced to just our disability or gender. I'm disabled, trans, and proud. Folks like me deserve the freedom to live our lives without fear, just like everyone else.

12

KHALID ABU DAWAS

Khalid Abu Dawas is a Palestinian activist, slam poet, and student at New York University.

MY FATHER IS PALESTINIAN AND WAS BORN IN A REFUGEE CAMP in Jordan. From the time I was young, he would tell me stories about the 1948 war and how his family fled to Jordan. More than 700,000 Palestinians were expelled from their homes in the Nakba, or the Catastrophe. He would tell me about sites, scents, and sounds in Palestine that he couldn't remember but that his grandfather recalled longingly. He talked of my grandfather's strength and my grandmother's resilience. They would split rice grain by grain, and receive one monthly ration of flour, rice, and eggs. Their home was a small shanty with three walls, barely strong enough to withstand the elements.

Those conversations with my father always went back to the Al-Aqsa Mosque in Jerusalem, one of the holiest sites in Islam.

He would show me videos of Al-Aqsa and tell me how the mosque was the center of Palestinian and Muslim life. Al-Aqsa called to him. It was calling to me, too, he said.

That feeling was incredibly powerful for me growing up. I didn't have a memory of this place, but I felt a deep connection to it. I hadn't been directly displaced, but felt like I was living in a diaspora. It was as though something was tugging on me, as though I felt attached elsewhere.

I was born in Anaheim, California, and raised in San Diego. I was an odd mix of culture and religion. My mother is European American and Catholic, and my father is Sunni Muslim. We celebrated both Christmas and Eid. I didn't learn Arabic growing up because my father worked long hours, seven days a week, and my mother didn't speak the language. I grew up listening to the Eagles and Umm Kulthum. I loved Arabic music! My dad would drive me to school, and when we'd pull in, he'd lower the windows and raise the volume. I felt embarrassed and proud. I was different, but had my own culture.

Halves and percentages didn't matter much to my father. Al-Nakba had fundamentally shaped his life, and he wanted to share that with his children. As I had heard stories about Palestine, and being both Palestinian and Muslim in America, I grasped at a very young age that it was going to be difficult as I got older. Nobody sat down and told me that, but I developed that understanding quickly. It cultivated in me a mindset of resistance and resilience. I'm forever grateful to my father for those conversations because they provided the foundation for my life and work today. It gave me the ability to absorb hate, move past it, and educate.

My activism in many ways began with my poetry. In middle school, I wrote about feelings of separation and how I felt disenfranchised. It wasn't definitively political; it was more about my fractured identity, being both mixed race and Palestinian. My writing turned explicitly political in high school. I wrote about the Nakba, my family's exodus from Palestine, and the diaspora. I was noticed locally and regionally, and was quickly adopted into the broader Muslim and Palestinian community. It was in their company that I learned how to celebrate Palestinian culture independent of the struggle. The injustices committed against our people didn't define us. We have a rich history that pre-existed the occupation and will endure after it; it's our responsibility to live this culture and share it with others.

In late high school, I visited Palestine. I didn't have a plan. I just wanted to explore. I traveled across the region and stayed with friends in cities that I had only read about. Nablus, Jenin, and Tulkarm were more stirring in real life than any picture could ever capture.

I realized then that it is fundamentally Palestinians who are determining their own destiny. We've seen other conflicts where impacted communities experience a kind of resignation or relocate. But not in Palestine. I met Palestinians who had been mistreated, harmed, or jailed, or had even lost loved ones, but would never leave their ancestral land. Palestinians will always take up their flag, and there will always be others to pick it up when it falls. They have decided to chart their own destiny, no matter what injustices are inflicted upon them.

It's become a way of life for Palestinians. They assume this mantle for other communities, too. Palestinians are constantly resisting injustice. We work towards building a better future every day for everyone.

I came to NYU in the fall of 2016 because I thought it would be a wonderful venue to expand my activism. It was a top school, located in a cosmopolitan city, with immense diversity. I expected to meet people like me, who were willing to put their life on the line for an important cause. I quickly realized that worldview wasn't common at NYU, and that the school didn't foster those values either. So I started exploring slam poetry both at NYU and across the city. I worked on issues relating to student debt, gentrification, LGBTQIA rights, and Black Lives Matter.

I also joined the Students for Justice in Palestine (SJP) chapter at NYU. SJP is an international anti-Zionist student activist organization with over 125 chapters in the United States that supports the Boycott, Divestment, and Sanctions Movement (BDS). BDS is a global campaign that seeks to increase economic, social, and political pressure on Israel to end long-standing violations of international law. The movement has drawn the ire of many universities, politicians, and Israel because of its success. Hundreds of resolutions have been passed worldwide in support of the campaign. Despite being a freshman, I worked hard to enhance the membership of SJP, expand our platform, build our reach, and collaborate with other organizations, including Black Lives Matter.

Across the country, SJP members and BDS activists routinely experience hate and bigotry on account of their activism and political beliefs. On January 31, 2017, SJP received an email from an anonymous IP address. The email threatened to disclose our members' immigration statuses, religious affiliations, and other personal information to U.S. and Israeli federal agencies. The message specifically targeted our Muslim and Arab members. It read:

> ATTENTION MUSLIMS, ARABS AND OTHER "ANTI-ZIONIST" CAMPUS TROLLS: Your names, image, friends list, postings, family member id's and other personal info. will be submitted— in conjunction with other collected data sets—and sent to the following Federal Agencies.

The agencies included the Justice Department, Immigration and Customs Enforcement, Department of Homeland Security, TSA, the states' attorneys general, local and state police agencies, and Israeli authorities.

The email also threatened to "crush" SJP chapters and BDS supporters at Rutgers University, Vassar College, UCLA, and the California State University system, in addition to Black Lives Matter and LGBTQIA groups that support Palestinian rights. The message concluded:

or our request that NYU be a sanctuary. He didn't even stand by us publicly. Our lives had been threatened and the university community didn't even know. If the impacted group had been any other community, including a Jewish student organization, the response would have been public, swift, and unequivocal.

An opportunity then fell into our laps. The Asian/Pacific/American Institute at NYU had launched a story project on hate incidents experienced by NYU students in the first one hundred days of the Trump administration. They wanted someone from our organization to share our story. Some in the organization felt trepidation, especially the non-citizens. They worried that a public video could cause us to be profiled or surveilled. Others thought that we should de-escalate. Some friends outside the organization warned me that participation in the video could cause me to lose housing or even be suspended or expelled. That's the pathology of power and submission. Abandon moral righteousness for fear of further wrongful reprisal.

I immediately stepped up. I wasn't afraid. I was worried about surveillance, but like many in our community, I was acclimated to it. When I was nine years old, a college bank account held under my name was frozen just because my dad was Palestinian Muslim. In Israel, I had been interrogated without cause so many times. I wanted to be a resource for people who felt unsafe. I wanted those who wished us harm to see my face and know that NYU SJP would not back down. This is why I had those conversations with my father. This is why I came to NYU.

The video was produced and widely shared, and brought additional, much-needed attention to the threat and the university's failed response. I personally received a lot of backlash. People would say abusive things as I walked by, give me angry looks, and send me hateful messages online. That's what happens when SJP students take a public stand and refuse to submit. I quickly became a name on campus.

We then received another round of death threats and violent warnings in April. Instead of a single email, this time we received

By the Sword of David, we will smash your collective skulls
together online, and shatter your futures to pieces. And,
Muzz/Arabs; It'll be a Family Affair for you. That is a promise y
may wish to meditate upon before ruining your family's lives.

The email shook our membership to the core. Some of
colleagues and friends were afraid for their lives. The timin
the threat is important. We received the email eleven days a
Trump was inaugurated, and just two days after Trump sig
the first Muslim travel ban. Authorities used that order to
gally detain hundreds of travelers and to profile thousands m
Hate violence against Muslims and Arabs was spiking as wel
was quite literally chaos, and many had already feared for t
safety. Now they felt like there was a target on their back. 1
was not free speech. It was a threat against our lives.

We were concerned for our undocumented friends. M;
were our allies and had supported our organization for ye;
Some of them were public about their immigration status.
didn't know what to expect from this administration, but
the rhetoric was a guide, our undocumented students could
at imminent risk of detention and deportation. Even our no
citizen members and allies were at risk. The travel ban h
already impacted NYU staff, faculty, and students. A red fl
in their student or immigration files could prevent them fro
reentering this country.

We called the campus public safety office, and they we
unhelpful. They said there was nothing they could do. Tl
NYPD said the same thing. It was obvious that nobody care
about the lives of anti-Zionist students, so we wrote a lett
to Andrew Hamilton, the president of NYU, and made thre
demands: that he voice unequivocal opposition to any threat
to students or student organizations, investigate the legit
macy of these threats, and declare NYU a sanctuary campu
immediately.

The response from Hamilton was shameful. He condemne
the email, but said nothing about the legitimacy of the threat

numerous private messages from three separate accounts via our Facebook account. The messages were sent from unidentifiable, alias accounts and targeted NYU SJP members, members of the Black Lives Matter movement, Palestinians, and Muslims, and urged us to stop all advocacy in support of Palestine. One message read in part:

> You will all be shhot [sic] at your next protest SJP members. It will be a family affair . . . WE WILL KILL ALL OF YOUR TROLLS WITH GUNS AT YOUR NEXT PROTEST YOU WILL ALL DIE WE WILL MURDER YOU ALL THE BLOOD WILL RUNS [sic] SLOWLY ON THE STREETS OF NYC . . . WE WILL PAINT THE STREET WITH PALESTINIAN/MUSLIM/BLACK LIVES MATTER/STUDENTS FOR JUSTICE IN PALESTINE/BLOOD . . .

and

> You will all die. If not today, then at your next protest.

Some of the messages were extremely graphic and referenced organs, mouths, butts, and intestines. Our response was the same. We notified our members, reached out to campus police and the NYPD, and made demands of the administration. We demanded that they circulate a statement to the entire NYU community saying that the university unequivocally opposes any threats to students and student organizations, recognizes the specific and repeated targeting of NYU SJP and its members, and reaffirms the right of students to advocate for justice in Palestine. We also demanded that they carry out an investigation of the legitimacy of these threats and meet with representatives of NYU SJP to discuss this harassment, and that President Hamilton declare NYU a sanctuary campus and implement all associated policies immediately.

Unlike the previous time, campus public safety took these threats more seriously, and it appeared that a meaningful investigation was under way. In addition, the university released a statement, but it was not circulated to the school. Instead, it was published quietly on the NYU website and signed by the university spokesman, not by Hamilton. It also took them five days to respond. The lag spoke volumes. It spoke of unease and distrust. How could there not be a prompt and strong public university response to death threats against students?

In response to the latest round of threats, we organized an event called "Here We Will Stay," titled after a poem by Palestinian poet Tawfiq Zayyad, in Washington Square Park, across the street from NYU. We wanted the university and others to know that we planned to stay the course and would never cower in the face of bigotry.

We won. Shortly before our event, we received an apology from an anonymous email account for all of the prior messages and death threats. The email said they disagreed with us, but that going forward they would leave us alone. It's now been many months, and we haven't received a single threat since that day. We showed the NYU community that we were a force on campus. We overcame this hateful chapter through conviction, perseverance, media advocacy, organizing, and our willingness to meet with the other side.

Although Palestinians, Arabs, Muslims, and BDS activists experience hate and bigotry regularly, I do believe that the political climate sparked these threats. One of the threats arrived right after the inauguration; the other set came just a few months later. I think Trump's rhetoric and discriminatory policies like the Muslim ban made people think they could express their most vile beliefs, which are often reserved for people in our community. Let's be matter-of-fact. There are many people and politicians in this country, including the president, who don't want people like me in this country. If they had their way, and there were no constitutional limits, I would be deported, banned, or have to register. I'm grateful that, in this case, the other side still had some modicum of humanity. When they saw our letters, faces, commitment to a discussion in Washington Square Park, and the pain we endured, I think they experienced a kind of course correction—not in their ideology, but in their tactics. It's not everything, but it's something.

When I think about hate on campus, I strongly believe that universities must treat all students equally. The suffering and pain of some can't be prioritized over others'. NYU brazenly ignored and disregarded public death threats to Muslim, Arab, and Palestinian students. To this day, the president has not met with us, nor has he publicly condemned the hate we received last academic year in a widely circulated statement signed by him. In this regard, any university that purports to stand for equality must also become a sanctuary for undocumented students. Undocumented students must not be left behind.

Universities must also foster different and difficult conversations on campus. One idea is a dialogue series, where vulnerable and impacted communities can share their stories. These open forums are critical, because so many students are misinformed or even undecided about how they feel about others. There will always be white supremacists and Zionists who want to discredit me because I'm a Palestinian Muslim. But there are so many in the undecided middle who can learn a great deal in an open forum. I still get asked, even in New York, if I support ISIS or beat my wife. We have a long way to go in educating one another. It's one of the reasons that I always make myself available to answer questions about Islam and Palestine. Every campus should host forums featuring marginalized communities, in particular undocumented and queer students.

In addition, universities must not use their faculty as a shield from criticism. In many cases, universities deflect criticisms about programming and diversity on campus by citing the growing diversity of their faculty. However, faculty members are often restrained in what they can say because of departmental or university politics. Others are desperate to just get tenure and avoid controversy at all costs. Numbers alone won't change anything.

I also believe that in fostering difficult conversations, universities must have clear and fair policies on who they sponsor and invite to speak on campus. My philosophy is to invite everybody or nobody. Universities get in trouble because they become partisan. They give one side a greater platform than the others. Universities love to host Zionist and pro-Israeli speakers, for example, but rarely do they ever sponsor the Palestinian perspective. In addition, many universities handpick the audience for controversial speakers or strictly regulate who can attend and ask questions. Many students would stop protesting alt-right and neo-Nazi speakers on campus if universities were more evenhanded about who they invited and who is permitted to participate.

Universities should also protect their students from unfair, discriminatory reputational harm. Some years ago, a group of people created Canary Mission, a database which purports to document people and organizations that are anti-Semitic and hate Israel. But it's really a doxing site that seeks to ruin the lives of pro-Palestinian activists. The site reveals private details about activists and discredits them based on false accusations, all in an effort to prevent them from securing employment. Many SJP members across the country are listed and experience discrimination and stigma because of it. Universities like NYU should take a stand against these McCarthy-ist watchlists that impact the employment prospects and emotional lives of their students.

As I look forward, I want to focus less on grandiose questions like how we fix America and more on how I can fix my community. I can't control what America thinks, but I can work to reform the community right in front of me. Every day is an opportunity. A chance to write, create, and build. We have so much agency in our own communities. Write a poem, provide a platform, convene a meeting. Do the little things. My daily act of resistance is wearing a *kufiyah*, a traditional Palestinian scarf. It puts me in constant dialogue with others and my own diaspora.

13

RUTH HOPKINS

Ruth Hopkins is a Native tribal attorney, judge, scientist, and writer. She was born on the Standing Rock Sioux Indian Reservation.

MY ENGLISH NAME IS RUTH HOPKINS, BUT MY REAL NAME IS Cankudutawin, Red Road Woman. I am Dakota and Lakota from the Occti Sakowin, otherwise known as the Great Sioux Nation. I was born in Fort Yates, North Dakota, on the Standing Rock Sioux Indian Reservation. I am an enrolled member of the Sisseton Wahpeton Dakota, who are located on the Lake Traverse Reservation at Fort Sisseton, South Dakota. I grew up on those two reservations, as well as at the Spirit Lake Nation at Fort Totten, North Dakota, and the Crow Creek Sioux Reservation at Fort Thompson, South Dakota.

I am assigned a number because the Great Sioux Nation was once at war with the U.S. The U.S. still monitors the tribe, holds my family's lands in trust, and tracks my lineage. My Dakota ancestors were exiled from Minnesota after the Dakota War of 1862, and the state put a bounty on the scalp of every Dakota man, woman, and child. The Lakota beat the U.S. in Red Cloud's War in 1868. The soldiers were so afraid of our warriors that they wanted a treaty to make peace with us. One of my ancestors signed that treaty. The U.S. later breached the Fort Laramie Treaty and stole the sacred Black Hills, but the U.S. Supreme Court ruled in *United States v. Sioux Nation of Indians* that the theft of the Black Hills was a wrongful taking. The Oceti Sakowin still own the sacred Black Hills, as long as the grass grows and the river flows.

I went off the reservation for college and graduate school. I'm both a scientist and a lawyer. I was a science professor for several years, and am now a tribal attorney and a judge. I've been called a journalist, activist, feminist, progressive, environmentalist, and radical. But if you ask me, I'm just an Oceti Sakowin woman like my grandmothers. I'm not a Republican or a Democrat. I follow my instincts. I protect the people and the sacred.

My identity as a Native woman is my birthright. It's all that I am. We were prayed into existence by the ones the colonizer could not kill. We carry the spirits of those who are older than time, and it is our turn to lead. We are responsible for preserving our Native languages, cultures, and belief systems, and for securing a future for the unborn and the next seven generations. This includes protecting the land and water. We are the new ancestors.

I first experienced race-based hate when I was five or six years old. It was laced with misogyny, as often happens. My mother took me to a border town to run errands and check the mail. Some old white men called me a squaw. I knew then that I was different from others.

Racism has been part of my life ever since. In seventh grade, I went to an off-reservation school because my father thought I would get a better education there. One of the teachers made a game out of guessing my race. It went on for weeks. At the start of class, he would look at me and say "Slavic?" "Latina?" and so on. I was the only Native in the class.

While I was at the University of North Dakota, I was assigned a teaching internship at a local upper-class high school. I was attacked in the hall by male athletes on my first day. They called me a "prairie nigger" and threw things at me. I was also attacked while protesting my university's mascot during a homecoming game because I believed the Fighting Sioux mascot encouraged racism and violence towards Native people. There were other incidents, too. I remember a college sorority throwing a Halloween party where they dressed up in skimpy "Indian" costumes. In a biology class, a fellow student called Winona LaDuke, a well-respected Native leader, a "dirty Indian." Another time I overheard girls calling the Indian Studies program "Idiot Studies." It was never-ending, and the administration did little to stop it. (Thanks to the work of strong Native activists at UND, though, the racist mascot was later abandoned.)

The list could go on forever.

The tumultuous relationship between the U.S. government and the Tribes is well documented. George Washington and Thomas Jefferson called for our extermination. Abraham Lincoln signed an order to hang thirty-eight of my Dakota ancestors at Mankato in the largest mass execution in U.S. history. Many Natives are fond of John F. Kennedy, but even he pushed through a dam that destroyed Native lands. While U.S. presidents haven't been openly hostile towards tribes in the past several decades, they have routinely refused to honor treaties and fulfill their trust obligations. Nixon was a surprisingly good president for Natives because he pushed for self-determination. The American Indian Movement forced his hand by descending on DC and occupying the Bureau of Indian Affairs.

Barack Obama has been the best president for Indian Country so far. He came to see us. I met him in Sioux Falls, South Dakota, along with other tribal leaders. Arvol Looking Horse, the Keeper of the Sacred White Buffalo Calf Pipe and my medi-cine man, came and blessed Obama. Natives always rely on their instincts. When we warm up to somebody, we treat them like family. By the end of the meeting, people were giving Obama blankets and hugging him. One big Indian put him in a head-lock and Obama's guard jumped! Obama laughed, though, because he was cool like that. We made strides with him. No other president acknowledged our history, rights, and humanity like he did. But I wish Obama had pardoned Native leader and activist Leonard Peltier. Leonard is a political prisoner who has been locked up for more than half his life. He was wrongfully convicted of murder, and Amnesty International, Nelson Man-dela, and many others have called for his release.

Trump is taking all this progress away. Only a few days after his inauguration, the Native American page, which detailed our liberties and rights, was removed from the White House web-site. Unlike some other pages, it was never reinstated. That was a sign of things to come.

In his first week, Trump paved the way for the Dakota Access Pipeline (DAPL) by signing an executive order forgoing an envi-ronmental assessment mandated by federal law. He also signed an order reviving the Keystone XL pipeline, a project Obama had vetoed. This was a declaration of war on Native communi-ties and an act of hate. Trump himself was an investor in the DAPL and openly advocated for the Keystone XL pipeline. Kel-cy Warren, the CEO of Energy Transfer Partners, the company behind DAPL, donated to Trump's campaign. Trump is in bed with Big Oil.

Trump also set his sights on removing protections for wildlife, and reducing or eliminating protected sacred sites. For example, Obama created a national monument in Bears Ears in Utah to celebrate its rich cultural history. In June 2017, the U.S. Secre-tary of the Interior proposed rolling back the borders of Bears Ears and making the land available to ranchers, farmers, and oil drillers.

The Trump administration has also slashed funding for tribal programs and health care, a treaty-promised right. Natives will die because of Trump.

He wants to privatize tribal lands. It's almost a continuance of the failed Dawes Act of 1887, which turned reservations into a patchwork and ruined tribal jurisdiction. Under federal law, if there is no land, there is no tribe. While we will continue to exist as a people, should Trump complete his goal of privatization, tribes will enter a termination phase where pieces of land are sold off for energy development by individuals. Nothing will be left for our grandchildren. We belong to the land. It is where our ancestors are buried. It is where our sacred sites are located, and where we pray and hold ceremony.

Trump cares more about corporations than about people. Neither he nor corporations have any interest in safekeeping our lives or communities. Now it's a different form of extermination and hate. Day by day, reservation by reservation, privatization, environmental degradation, and corporate exploitation further Tribal termination. Trump, after all, routinely praises Andrew Jackson, the president who forced the Trail of Tears upon Native communities, killing thousands.

Our ancestors always told us that the occupiers would come back for more because Native lands are resource-rich and sacred. We leave the land undisturbed and keep the resources where they lie. Standing Rock was just the latest example of native resistance, a struggle dating back centuries.

Being both a scientist and a lawyer, I know the dangers of Big oil. The original Keystone pipeline crosses by the Lake Traverse Reservation and began operations in July 2010. Oil later spilled over land, and the corporations never cleaned it up. The penalties and regulations in place aren't strong enough to check Big oil companies. If there's a leak, they'll pay pennies. It's cheaper for them to break the law than to protect the environment.

That's why I opposed the Keystone XL pipeline. I couldn't bear the thought of it crossing the Ogallala Aquifer and poisoning the water source of millions of people, Native and non-Native. If oil spills into a water source, the water becomes polluted with toxins and is never the same. President Obama was right to stop construction of the pipeline in 2015 using a presidential veto.

We opposed construction of the Dakota Access Pipeline because it would have gone under Lake Oahe and the Missouri River, the primary water sources for the Standing Rock and Cheyenne River Reservations. Any contamination of this precious water source could force us from our lands. The DAPL would have also included known burial sites and land that clearly fell within the boundaries of the Fort Laramie treaty. It would violate our way of life and legal sovereignty.

In July 2016, Dakota Access started drilling without a permit. Only Native media organizations covered the story initially. Then the tribal chairman of Standing Rock and a member of the Standing Rock Tribal Council were arrested. The Native community decided this was an ancestral struggle. We were prepared to die to stop the pipeline. The original DAPL resistance camps were Sacred Stone, first, and then Red Warrior. The largest camp would come to be named after the Oceti Sakowin. It later became known as the Big Camp and was created in August 2016.

It was personal to me because I was born at Standing Rock and am both Dakota and Lakota descending from the Oceti Sakowin. I have family and friends there, and my father has land there, too. It's been in our family since the treaty days. My tribe had its own camp within Oceti Sakowin. I lived about three hours away, and made several trips back and forth from the camp. It was really something to see a few dozen people there one week and many thousands just a few weeks later. For a time, all the Native Nations were represented at Standing Rock. There was a true spirit of unity and solidarity. A lot of non-Natives from all over the world showed up, too. This fight spoke to the heart and soul of so many. It was as though we were all being called home.

We stayed unarmed throughout the resistance. We knew if any of us carried a weapon, they would use it as an excuse to kill us, just as they did at Wounded Knee in 1890, when U.S. soldiers used a single shot fired in their direction as justification for killing three hundred Lakota people. We nevertheless prepared for an invasion, and the children were taught an escape route, in case the adults were taken.

I wasn't there for the Day of the Dogs, on September 3. Dakota Access learned that there were burial sites along their proposed route and immediately started bulldozing there. They wanted to destroy the evidence. Standing Rock elders and historians had pointed to burial markers on that site. Dakota Access had also destroyed burial sites during earlier construction and should have been fined because of it. When water protectors at camp saw this, they put their bodies on the line, in the path of the bulldozer. Most of them were women and children. Dakota Access had hired mercenaries with vicious dogs to ensure that construction of the pipeline could continue at the site. Amy Goodman, the host of *Democracy Now!*, captured footage of dogs with bloodied mouths running down water protectors. A pregnant woman was bitten. After it was viewed more than fourteen million times, Goodman was arrested on a riot charge for covering the incident, but was later exonerated.

Then there was the Treaty Camp raid in October. That's when they tore up a sacred Native sweat lodge and dragged people out in the middle of the ceremony. This marked the beginning of the mass arrests. One hundred and forty-two people from that small resistance camp were arrested that day alone. There was extreme police brutality. Protesters were pepper-sprayed, beaten, and shot with rubber bullets. Police also used sound canons and flash grenades. That's when they took the indigenous activist Red Fawn. She was wrongly accused of using a firearm that day. They still have her.

The assault on Backwater Bridge took place from November 20 to November 21. It's still hard to talk about. It started on a Sunday. Law enforcement from multiple states were there, along with paid mercenaries. They were completely militarized and looked like they were going to war. They were wearing protective gear and armed to the max, but you could tell that some of them were afraid. They were scared of unarmed, praying, tired, cold, unwashed Natives and their allies. Day turned to night. Police sprayed people with water cannons when the temperature was below freezing. Even if you weren't in the front, you were still sprayed with an icy mist. It chilled you to the bone. I was wearing jeans under a long skirt with a hoodie and a hat and my face was covered, but I was still freezing. The grass turned into little blades of ice. I heard one officer say, "Water is life," as they sprayed civilians down with ice water. They were mocking us. Our rallying cry throughout the resistance was *Mni wiconi*. Water is life. They had weaponized water.

Police were Macing everyone who came close. They shot people with rubber bullets. They aimed for women's genitals and laughed about it. The cold water and pepper spray were traumatic and shocking. Some people urinated on themselves. That was the night they shot Sophia Wilansky. Sophia almost lost her arm. It's still not fully functional and requires more surgery. They shot Vanessa Dundon that night, too. She was working security at the camp, and nearly lost an eye. Hundreds of others were injured.

I was exposed to something that night. I still don't know what it was, but I had nosebleeds regularly for six months afterwards. I had previously gone years without a single nosebleed.

I quickly left the area so I could share the video footage and information, to help get the word out. My Twitter account and the footage trended nationwide the next day. Millions saw it.

Within a few weeks, President Obama saw things our way and decided that Dakota Access had to complete a full environmental impact statement and consider alternative routes before proceeding with further construction. People celebrated that day. They danced and called it a victory. Obama should have arrived at this decision earlier, like he did with Keystone XL.

Some of us knew it wasn't over, though. Sure enough, Trump approved the pipeline just after taking office, along with the Keystone XL. The remaining water protectors were driven from camp during the last raid in February 2017. They arrested Regina Brave, a woman some call The Grandmother Who Resisted; she was at the Occupation of Wounded Knee in 1973. Activists involved in the movement are still being stalked, harassed, and surveilled.

Natives living today survived genocide. Some tribes were completely wiped out; many had a population decrease of 90 percent or more. I know a few tribes who consist of only one family. When you look at our history, the mere fact that we're still alive and holding onto our cultures, languages, and identities is resistance. Resistance takes many forms for us because we're under attack in so many ways, including government and corporate encroachment, environmental destruction, dismantling of tribal sovereignty, police violence, and the disappearance and murder of Native women.

Cheyenne River has a camp to fight the Keystone XL pipeline. The Apache seek to protect Oak Flat. Tribes along the Mexican border are fighting Trump's wall, which would cut through their lands. Natives are more likely to be harmed or killed by police violence than any other community. Five Natives were killed by police in October 2017, and a fourteen-year-old Native boy, Jason Pero, was murdered by a police officer just last week. One in three Native women will have been raped in her lifetime. I am one of those Native women. Most men who commit sexual violence against Native women are non-Native. This epidemic continues to worsen because reservations do not have jurisdiction over non-Natives. We must raise awareness about these gross abuses.

Resistance is also making babies and raising them to be healthy Natives who love themselves and each other. It's rising past decades of forced assimilation and historical trauma and making our voices heard. It's getting an education, and escaping the crushing poverty that has been imposed upon us, without compromising who we are. It's telling our stories. It's exercising our hunting and fishing rights. It's the determination to carry on. Our existence is resistance against colonialism and the false system that seeks to separate us from ourselves, each other, Mother Earth, and *Wakantanka* (the Great Mystery).

As I speak, there are Natives studying to become teachers, doctors, and lawyers. There are Natives learning their language and singing in their Native tongue while drumming. Some are beading. Others are at camps all over the country that continue to fight Big oil. We were born to fight. It's in our blood. The front line is everywhere.

Allies can help by boosting Native voices. Follow us and read our work. Buy our goods and services, and support Native businesses and artisans. Educate yourself on the real history of the U.S. and support our causes. Don't wear ridiculous, stereotypical "Indian costumes." They're degrading and disrespectful. Believe in climate change and fight against it. Fight corporate abuse and excess, especially when it targets Mother Earth. Reject corporate–state militarism and police violence, and stand up for women. Show up at our rallies, call your elected officials, and don't vote for politicians who want to exterminate and destroy our way of life. See us. Hear us. Make sure we are included. Don't speak over us. Every time another one of us connects back to the sacred hoop, we win.

CONCLUSION

HOPE IN A TIME OF DESPAIR

AMERICA MEANS DIFFERENT THINGS TO DIFFERENT PEOPLE. Asmaa Albukaie found refuge in Boise, Idaho, after losing her husband, and nearly losing her two children, in the Syrian civil war. She will forever be grateful to this country for giving her family a second chance. Ruth Hopkins was born on Standing Rock, and many of her Native ancestors were dispossessed and exterminated to make room for a new nation. Officers in uniform from that same nation then assaulted her hundreds of years later because they wanted what little her community has left. There is no elixir to cure bigotry and hate in America because it runs so deep in our history, and individuals and communities experience it very differently. But I observed commonalities among survivors and their communities that should inform our analysis going forward.

Survivors' and Community Needs

Survivors need a stronger safety net to heal and move past hate. They have both acute and long-term needs, ranging from the physical and the emotional to financial concerns and personal safety. They have to pay medical bills, take time off from work, have difficult conversations with friends and family, and, in some cases, require additional security. In the wake of hate, they are thrust into a terrifying spotlight; looking on are law enforcement, lawyers, the media, and the public. In addition to bearing any physical injuries, survivors often experience mental health issues and suffer from post-traumatic stress disorder (PTSD), depression, anxiety, and anger.[1] As we have seen in this book, it does not take bodily injury to cause this dislocation. Research shows that hate crime survivors feel more vulnerable and fearful than do victims of other crimes. The recovery period can be twice as long.[2]

Survivors deserve to be healthy and happy. None of them should have to struggle to meet basic needs, or to access health care and mental health support. Many lack either one or both because they are recent immigrants, who may struggle with the language and may not have the necessary means and resources. Cities and localities should fund and appoint advocates drawn from vulnerable communities to support survivors. These advocates can help survivors access health care and resources, engage with law enforcement, navigate the legal system, respond to press inquiries, and assist with financial planning and fundraising campaigns set up on their behalf. Authorities should also set aside rapid-response funding so that they are able to address acts of hate when they occur. Having a separate pool of money designated expressly for this purpose will allow officials to more effectively meet the needs of survivors and their communities. They should likewise support the creation of local task forces and other collectives so that there is meaningful infrastructure in place to help.

Survivors need to know that they are not alone. When I sat down with them in their communities, many talked about feeling isolated, out of place, and forgotten. After the cameras leave, the phone calls slow, and the letters of support stop, they find themselves struggling. Many of the people profiled in this book expressed a strong interest in meeting one another, hearing and sharing one another's stories, and healing together. We have support groups for so many different communities in this country, including victims of gun violence, family members with incarcerated loved ones, and people recovering from substance abuse and drug addiction. But there are few if any support groups for hate crime survivors. They would be a timely and much-needed intervention.

We must also be attentive to the needs of vulnerable communities at large. The vandalism and arson of houses of worship, and the targeting of organizations, student groups, and campus communities, together with state-sponsored forms of hate (such as mass deportations and police brutality), impact entire communities. Even hate crimes that target individuals send community-wide messages that its members are not welcome, and undermine feelings of safety and security. Researchers call it the "vicarious traumatization effect": communities experience some of the same emotions and struggles as individual survivors.[3]

Healing and restoring affected communities is critical because there is a growing body of evidence showing the devastating consequences of racism and hate. Hate makes communities physically and emotionally sick. Racism literally debilitates and kills. It can affect blood pressure and cortisol levels, and lead to a greater likelihood of obesity, decreased immune function, cancer, or death.[4] This is especially true when the affected community has previously experienced abuse and discrimination, because members relive that trauma and pass it on from generation to generation. A recent study found that black women are roughly two to three times more likely to die from pregnancy- and childbirth-related causes than white women.[5] Variables like education and wealth do not matter, meaning that economic

interventions are not enough.[6] Hate is a public health issue, and
the government should fund research and treat it like one.

Sharing and discussion are a vital step in moving past hate.
In the wake of recent hate incidents, several communities have
convened public town halls. After a racist note threatening violence was left outside a black-owned hair salon in Elk Grove,
California, community members discussed hate that targeted
black, Latinx, and Asian communities and police profiling and
bullying of their youth.[7] After an elementary school was vandalized with anti-black graffiti in Bucks County, Pennsylvania,
parents discussed how to talk about racism and hate with their
children.[8] Public town halls like these are educational, cathartic,
and empowering. Programming is also important. After hateful vandalism on school property and fear among students that
their parents could be deported, the superintendent of schools in
Contra Costa County, California, created "Allies & Advocates,"
an initiative intended to foster racial equity, inclusion, and social
justice in the classroom.[9] Again, cities and localities should support these town halls and programming through already set-
aside rapid response funding. Legislators can likewise mirror
these efforts and convene open hearings where survivors and
community leaders can share their stories and provide input on
best practices to curb hate. Work done in the name of survivors
must center them—their needs and their experiences.

Focusing on communities is additionally important because
we know that the majority of hate incidents and hate crimes go
unreported.[10] Many survivors distrust the police, fear shaming
and retaliation, worry about surveillance, or are uncomfortable
sharing personal details with law enforcement, including their
immigration status or sexual orientation.[11] Many people withhold information, lie, or even alter their identity because they
worry about their safety. Just in this book, we learned about
a Muslim girl forced to give up her hijab (chapter 10), a trans
man who now rarely publicly identifies as trans (chapter 11), and
a Muslim boy who wondered whether he should lie about his

faith (chapter 1). There is no substitute for community-wide support, because it allows us to reach the survivors we know and those we do not.

Community Activists and Local Organizations

Everyone must do their part to prevent, identify, document, and respond to hate. Community activists and local organizations have always led this work and will do so in the future. They work directly with marginalized communities, support survivors, raise awareness, develop policy, combat criminalization, and serve as a resource for local and federal lawmakers. They often do so behind the scenes, with limited resources and capacity. In 2017 alone, activists and organizations planned vigils, community conversations, know-your-rights presentations, teach-ins, and rallies on issues ranging from the Muslim ban, refugee rights, immigration raids, and police brutality to affordable health care, access to abortion, and climate change. In the absence of reliable statistics about the prevalence of hate, they also collect data about hate incidents against their communities.

Activists are building coalitions spanning multiple communities and issues, without flattening the great diversity of experience within those communities. We have seen extraordinary examples of solidarity and racial justice in the wake of Trump's election. Japanese Americans have stood with Muslims and refugees to condemn the travel bans because they know that history rhymes.[12] Native communities have worked closely with Latinx communities to oppose the southern border wall because they believe in open and free borders, not in colonial and arbitrary ones.[13] And undocumented youth from the brown, black, and Asian American Pacific Islander communities have joined forces in supporting DACA, TPS, and the clean Dream Act because they know that immigration enforcement is racialized.[14]

We have seen powerful examples of solidarity in this book, too.

Marwan Kreidie (chapter 7) recommended that mosques serve as sanctuaries for undocumented immigrants, and described how United Voices, an advocacy group in Philadelphia, creates opportunities for vulnerable communities to share their stories, educate others, and meet with lawmakers. Sarath Suong (chapter 6) discussed the many groups that PrYSM serves, including Southeast Asians, the queer community, and survivors of police violence, and how they helped pass one of the most progressive civil rights and anti-violence ordinances in the country. Tanya Gersh (chapter 8) described how she has come to feel a close connection to the mothers of black, Latinx, Muslim, and queer children, and wants to build community alongside them. Khalid Abu Dawas and the Students for Justice in Palestine chapter at New York University (chapter 12) responded to violent threats with a list of demands, including urging New York University to become a sanctuary campus.

Groups that focus on racial equity and justice must center Native and black voices in their work. This country was built on the decimation of these communities, and everyday anti-Native and black racism is its unavoidable legacy. The closer these communities are to liberation, the closer we all are.[15] We must also confront discrimination and bias in our own communities, and ensure that individuals who are members of multiple vulnerable communities are respected and included. Too often we treat these issues as taboo and self-divide and conquer, leaving us unable to challenge a system that deprives us all. A 2016 open letter, "Dear Mom, Dad, Uncle, Auntie: Black Lives Matter to Us, Too," is a powerful example of youth challenging generational bias. The letter is from Asian and South Asian young people to their elders, and urges them to confront and abandon anti-black bias and to "empathize with the anger and grief of the fathers, mothers, and children who have lost their loved ones to police violence."[16]

Communities must ultimately decide what will keep them safe. They cannot necessarily look to the state and its institutions as a solution, because much of the violence they endure comes at the hands of the state. Instead, community groups must consider to what degree they can complement, supplement, or even replace traditional law enforcement, or, in some cases, serve as a defense against them. In the wake of hate, we have seen organizations like PrYSM recommit to self-defense classes, colleague and buddy check-ins, and neighborhood watch programs. Desis Rising Up & Moving, a multi-generational grassroots organization led by low-wage South Asian immigrant workers and youth in New York City, helped form Hate Free Zones in Jackson Heights and Kensington, and is coordinating programming that includes self-defense classes, bystander intervention training, and a rapid response plan to combat immigration raids.[17] More than eight hundred churches, including the Southside Presbyterian Church in Tucson, Arizona, Iglesia de Dios Pentecostal in New Haven, Connecticut, and the First Unitarian Society in Denver, Colorado, have given sanctuary to undocumented immigrants seeking safety from raids, detention, and deportation.[18] Many groups are also leveraging technology to protect their most vulnerable. *Notifica* allows undocumented immigrants who are detained to send pre-loaded personal messages to friends and family with the press of a single panic button.[19] *RedadAlertas* gathers verified and crowdsourced data on immigration raids and the like and delivers it to communities, organizers, journalists, and others nearby.[20]

National Organizations and Allies

The work of local organizations is complemented by the work of national organizations, some of which are profiled in this book. The Southern Poverty Law Center has long documented and fought hate in America. It represents survivors like Tanya Gersh in litigation, and it profoundly served affected communities after the election by recording and tracking hate incidents across the country (chapter 8). The National Domestic Workers Alliance advocates for respect, fairness, and recognition for domestic workers, and has fought for sanctuary policies nationwide, alongside Jeanette Vizguerra (chapter 4). The National Women's Law Center fights for equality and opportunity for girls, women, and families, and documented an increase in sexual assault in the wake of the election, including through hotlines that Alexandra Brodsky (chapter 5) helped staff. The Center for Disability Rights supports and advocates for people with disabilities in all facets of their lives, including their civil and human right to health care, a cause that Dominick Evans (chapter 11) has championed in both his personal and professional lives.

Since the election, we have seen the single largest mobilization in American history. An estimated four million people took to the streets of DC and in more than 650 towns and cities across the country for the first Women's March.[21] We've also seen the birth of Indivisible, a political advocacy group that now has more than six thousand registered groups across the country, roughly six times the membership of the Tea Party at its peak.[22] The MeToo movement has drawn an important spotlight on the everyday sexism, misogyny, harassment, and assault that women continue to endure and helped foster the Time's Up initiative, which includes a legal defense fund to support less privileged women who experience sexual misconduct. People are connecting, organizing, and building community across this country, while condemning all manners of mistreatment. Unions, the interfaith community, and small and large businesses have joined the fight as well. Lawyers, too, have played an important role, and filed hundreds of lawsuits against the Trump administration. Their most important victories include helping to strike down portions of the Muslim ban and protecting federal funding to sanctuary cities.

National organizations, allies, and local communities must continue to center impacted communities, let them tell their own stories, and be guided by their needs and leadership. An important example is Communities Against Hate, a partnership between numerous local and community organizations (including the Arab Community Center for Economic and Social Services, Asian Americans Advancing Justice, Muslim Advocates, National Disability Rights Network, National Network for Arab American Communities, South Asian Americans Leading Together, and the Transgender Law Center), and several national organizations like The Leadership Conference Education Fund, Lawyers' Committee for Civil Rights Under Law, and the Southern Poverty Law Center. Together, these groups are documenting and capturing incidents of hate violence through an online database and telephone hotline and connecting survivors and witnesses to legal resources and social services.[23] Another successful collaboration is the NoMuslimBanEver campaign, a grassroots effort to raise awareness and resist and dismantle the Muslim and refugee bans. Community organizations lead the campaign and have held dozens of events across the country, while nearly two hundred organizations, many of them national, have formally endorsed the effort, lent their support on social media, and helped spread the word through their networks.[24]

Teachers, sports coaches, community liaisons, public health professionals, civic leaders, and other professionals should also develop programming to foster equity and inclusion in their communities. If local communities want to learn about marginalized communities, they should invite them to their schools, universities, workplaces, and houses of worship. Every manner in which we gather and convene provides an opportunity to learn and foster awareness. Do not wait for hate to strike. The people of Wausau, Wisconsin, for example, banded together for a "Community after Charlottesville" town hall because they wanted to be ready if hate groups planned a march in their community.[25] Programming, like community discussions and presentations by affected communities, stops hate from metastasizing. This programming should also include training for what bystanders can do, or what people who might want to intervene can do, so that we can live up to the examples set by Ricky Best and Taliesin

Myrddin Namkai-Meche in Portland (chapter 10) and Heather Heyer in Charlottesville. These networks can also be mobilized after hate crimes occur to support survivors and communities.

In that vein, this book provides many examples of what communities can do in the wake of a hate crime. They can hold community events celebrating life, organize rallies and other acts of solidarity condemning hate and bigotry, and directly support survivors through charitable giving. They can also engage the media and lawmakers.[26] They can write a letter to the editor or an essay for their local newspaper, issue a statement of support, and call upon school boards, city councils, and other officials to pass resolutions and bills that meaningfully take on hate.[27] There is no one-size-fits-all solution. Local communities must consult with survivors, follow their lead, and decide what is best given their collective and historical experiences.

Local communities face a similar choice, if and when white supremacists, anti-Muslim outfits, and other hate mongers come to town. We have seen dozens of such rallies since Trump took office, just like Charlottesville's, and can expect more in the future. In response, communities can hold counter rallies, events celebrating equity and justice, and support local organizations that fight bigotry on a daily basis. Communities must also understand that impacted persons may choose not to participate because they see these rallies as an important moment for white America to take a stand. Black Lives Matter organizers in Nashville, for example, decided not to join protests against planned white supremacist "White Lives Matter" rallies in Shelbyville and Murfreesboro in 2017 because they believed it was critical for white allies to exercise leadership and ownership in that moment.[28]

Finally, activists, advocates, and their organizations must pause and be responsive to their own trauma.[29] Many of us who work with affected communities are caught in an endless cycle of rapid response and crisis intervention, and do not have the time or resources for self-care. When we hear the stories of survivors, we absorb their pain. When we fight for their rights, we become an extension of their struggle. That is what happens when you work on the front lines. This is especially true if you come from a vulnerable community, as many of us do. I felt this acutely while working on this book. I sometimes felt alone and isolated, and had difficulty sharing my feelings. There were times when nothing would give me comfort, apart from being outside with our two family German shepherds. When I did want resources, I did not know where to turn. Individuals know their needs best, but it is incumbent on the rest of us to make sure that they have the resources to pause, heal, and recommit. This means equipping organizations with sufficient funding so that advocates can accept fellowships and take sabbaticals and significant time away. It also means supporting community artists who, through music, humor, dance, and multimedia, can provide powerful expressions of healing and restoration.

Lawmakers and Police

The federal government can make a difference by making the elimination of hate crimes a national priority. For example, in the wake of numerous attacks on African American churches in the 1990s, President Clinton declared the investigation and prevention of church arsons a national priority. He demanded that the government bring the culprits to justice, rebuild the houses of worship, and prevent additional crimes from occurring.[30] Within four years, the number of attacks on African American churches dropped by 53 percent.[31] Although the Trump administration would never make combating hate violence a national priority, it should be a priority for future administrations.[32]

Still, legislative efforts to reduce hate will have little enduring effect if the government continues to profile and criminalize vulnerable communities. Policies that criminalize or withhold rights from vulnerable communities both here and abroad intensify bigotry and hate. They reaffirm narratives of privilege and bias and reinforce dangerous stereotypes, causing communities to recoil and retreat, exacerbating their vulnerability. If the government stigmatizes us, so will others. Watchlists, suspicious activity reporting, countering violent extremism (CVE) programs, and the Department of Justice's racial-profiling guidelines treat Muslims, Arabs, South Asians, and refugees collectively with suspicion. Black and Native communities endure disproportionate police violence, arbitrary arrest, and incarceration, and members of Latinx communities are regularly profiled, detained, and subject to raids and deportation. And that was all happening before Trump.[33] These programs and policies have intensified under his watch. We have also seen the rescission of bathroom rules for transgender students and Title IX protections for survivors of sexual assault; the revival of anti-abortion policies; the rolling back of Department of Justice consent decrees and other police reforms; the theft and exploitation of Native-owned lands; and repeated attempts to repeal the Affordable Care Act.

The same is true for our international dealings. It should come as no surprise that drone strikes and extrajudicial killings are used principally in Muslim-majority countries against Muslims, that Guantanamo Bay has always been and continues to be a prison for Muslim men, and that climate change has hit the global south the hardest, with six of the top ten most-affected nations located in Africa.[34] Our efforts to reduce criminalization must be inclusive, anti-imperialist, and internationalist. Dr. Martin Luther King, Jr., articulated this vision best in his 1967 speech "Beyond Vietnam: A Time to Break Silence," in which he warned of "the giant triplets of racism, extreme materialism, and militarism," and urged a revolution in values, a spiritual awakening, and a united front to combat domestic and international deprivation.[35]

It is often said that conservatives define bigotry in terms of intention, and liberals define it in terms of impact. That may at times be a fair distinction, but it has collapsed under the Trump administration. We do not need to guess what Trump thinks about our communities, because he reminds us every chance he gets: Mexicans are "criminals" and "rapists"; Syrians are "snakes" and "could be ISIS"[36]; and refugees are "the ultimate Trojan horse."[37] "You have people coming out of mosques with hatred and death in their eyes."[38] He makes jokes about "Pocahontas" instead of honoring Native heroes. This is why communities increasingly experience criminalization and deprivation as state-sponsored forms of hate. These policies are inspired by bigotry and malice, and they disproportionately affect our communities and lead to citizen hate and violence.

Best practices for policing vulnerable communities has formed the basis of entire treatises, and this book cannot do justice to them all. The government must at a minimum follow basic standards, including due process, individualized suspicion, and evidence of wrongdoing. They must revisit what conduct is criminalized under the law, as well as exceptions to the law, and end the human rights atrocity of mass incarceration. A good litmus test is whether the policy in question would be acceptable if it disproportionately impacted white people. Over criminalization, police brutality, the Muslim and refugee bans, and mass deportations, for example, would fail this test because they disproportionately affect communities of color. Indeed, this is why the opioid epidemic is being treated as a public-health crisis rather than as a criminal justice one. Criminalizing opioids would entail the incarceration of many white Americans, an unacceptable outcome for lawmakers.

Lawmakers may not be able to change this architecture overnight, but they can publicly condemn these unfair policies and draw a clearer connection between criminalization, deprivation, and hate. When lawmakers condemn hate violence, they should simultaneously disavow policies that reinforce hate, bigotry, sexism, and white supremacy. They should also hold one another accountable for racist and xenophobic rhetoric, which can have deadly consequences. Local lawmakers can do their part by promulgating stronger civil rights protections than the federal government's and refusing to cooperate with overreaching federal authorities. We have seen states and localities provide sanctuary, oppose registries, and refuse to cooperate with counter-terrorism task forces. California governor Jerry Brown, for example, has pardoned undocumented immigrants who committed crimes in the state of California and thereby prevented their deportation.[39] The mayor of Oakland, Libby Schaaf, alerted city residents to imminent immigration raids so that they could be ready and prepared. In addition, many colleges and universities have declared themselves sanctuary campuses, including Columbia University, Wesleyan University, Portland State University, Oregon State University, Reed College, and California State University.[40] In some cases, community activists, advocates, and organizations sprang into action after Trump was elected and secured many of these victories.

Lawmakers must also tackle the threat of white supremacy in America. The greatest threat facing this country is homegrown white nationalists, not Muslims or refugees.[41] Hundreds of hate groups openly espouse white supremacy and other vile beliefs in this country, and their ranks are growing.[42] A joint FBI and Department of Homeland Security 2017 intelligence bulletin warned that white supremacist groups had already carried out more attacks than any other domestic extremist group over the past sixteen years and were likely to carry out more attacks over the coming year.[43] And yet lawmakers remain fixated on ISIS and other foreign extremist elements, rather than on the white supremacists who target us here at home.

But in responding to this threat, lawmakers must not commit the same harms on these communities they did on vulnerable communities. Dozens of human rights, civil liberties, and community advocacy organizations, for example, have repeatedly condemned CVE programs, which ask Muslim American leaders to identify Muslims who are at risk of becoming violent extremists.[44] These programs profile Muslim youth, chill civil liberties, and are a disguised form of predictive policing and surveillance.[45] These same advocacy organizations, in turn, wisely condemned the use of these programs to combat white supremacy after Charlottesville.[46] Equal-opportunity profiling and surveillance still infringes upon civil rights and will not make us safer. It also opens the door to these programs being repurposed to target other vulnerable communities. We recently learned that CVE programs are now being used to target black activists across the country.[47]

Lawmakers must likewise ensure that hate crime laws are robust and responsive to community needs. Hate crime laws are intended to respond to bias-motivated crimes, and have often been justified on the grounds that they can add time to criminal sentences.[48] But the real value of hate crime laws lies not in lengthy sentences and exacerbating mass incarceration. They are valuable because hate crimes have a deep and long-lasting impact on survivors, communities, and the public at large. It is thus critical for authorities to treat hate crimes differently from other crimes and to show vulnerable communities and the public at large that hate will not be tolerated. Furthermore, calling bias-motivated crimes hate crimes allows us to see these acts as related and interconnected, rather than as isolated events, which in turn provides an important opportunity to discuss the origins and proliferation of hate. Jurisprudence that focuses on motives like hate also allows judges and other decision makers to prescribe restorative sentences, like requiring offenders to learn about and volunteer with targeted communities. As part of a settlement agreement between Dyne Suh and a former Airbnb host who discriminated against her for being Asian, for example, the California Department of Fair Employment and Housing ordered the former host to take a course in Asian American studies.[49]

There are presently five states with no hate crime laws: Arkansas, Georgia, Indiana, South Carolina, and Wyoming.[50] Other states have laws but, in some cases, they cover only misdemeanors or exclude certain characteristics, like sex, sexual orientation, gender identity, and disability. The majority of hate crime prosecutions are brought at the state level, and so lawmakers must ensure that every state has a strong hate crime law that covers all protected characteristics and all manners of offenses.[51]

We also need a strong federal hate crime law to ensure that state prosecutors sufficiently investigate and try hate crime cases. Local prosecutors are less likely to turn a blind eye to hate violence if they know the federal government can step in and prosecute. To do so, Congress must revise its current federal hate crime law, the Matthew Shepard Act, passed in October 2009. As a result of a controversial court decision in 2011, courts increasingly require prosecutors to show that hate was the sole factor motivating the crime, not just a substantial motivating factor.[52] Under this logic, if a suspect vandalizes a synagogue because he hates Jews, but also dislikes the traffic that its presence leads to in his neighborhood, it may not be a hate crime.[53]

This is why activists have long believed that the Department of Justice refused to bring hate crime charges after the murders of Deah Shaddy Barakat, Yusor Mohammad Abu-Salha, and Razan Mohammad Abu-Salha in Chapel Hill, North Carolina, in February 2015. The three Muslim Americans were murdered, two of them execution-style, by a man who hated Muslims. But because he also had a long-standing parking dispute with the victims, he was not charged with a hate crime.[54] Congress can remedy this anomaly by passing legislation clarifying that bias need only be a substantial motivating factor in a hate crime, not the sole factor.

In addition, Congress must make hate crime reporting mandatory, rather than voluntary. The FBI releases an annual report on hate crimes, but it derives its data from voluntary and incomplete reporting by local law enforcement. A recent study by the Associated Press, for example, found that roughly 17 percent of all city and county law enforcement agencies did not bother to submit a single hate crime report from 2009 to 2014.[55] Another study by ProPublica found that 88 percent of agencies that filed a report in 2016 reported zero hate crimes.[56] Better data will allow us to see trends, including who is being targeted, where, and by whom, which will allow the government and communities to more effectively target their resources and outreach.

Mandatory reporting will likewise help keep police officers accountable. Some officers fail to investigate crimes as motivated by bias, or know very little about vulnerable communities. Only twelve states require police to learn how to identify and investigate hate crimes in the academy, and few agencies provide such training after they leave the academy.[57] For example, although the FBI began collecting data in 2015 on hate crimes committed against Sikhs, Arabs, and Hindus, local officials never received meaningful federal training about these communities.[58] Police officers cannot accurately report hate crimes if they do not know who is being attacked and why. That is why, according to the FBI, there were only seven hate crimes committed against Sikhs in the United States in 2016, even though community organizations believe there were many more and, in one case, recorded fifteen legal intakes from Sikh community members that same year.[59] In other cases, officers seek to brush hate aside or even harbor racist beliefs themselves, sentiments that are sometimes echoed by trainers who work closely with them across the country. It has been well documented, for example, that individuals affiliated with the Islamophobia industry—a vast network of junk scientists and think tanks that peddle dangerous falsehoods about Muslims—have long trained law enforcement on how to engage with Muslim communities.[60] Officers who hold prejudicial views or disproportionately target vulnerable communities are unlikely to report hate crimes unless they are required to do so.

Media

The media plays a critical role in the fight against hate because they keep elected officials and other decision makers informed and accountable. In the wake of the 2016 election, ProPublica launched "Documenting Hate," a national database to track hate crimes and bias incidents in America.[61] They have also worked closely with MuckRock, a nonprofit, collaborative news site committed to government transparency, to learn more about gaps and best practices in hate crime reporting. These efforts are critical because there is no reliable data documenting the prevalence of hate in America.

Reporters and others who cover hate must strike a delicate balance and at once center survivors and respect their privacy. This means giving them an opportunity to tell their stories, but also respecting their decision not to share. Stalking of survivors is unacceptable. Reporters have rules of ethics and codes of conduct for engaging subjects, including those experiencing trauma.[62] They should follow these rules when meeting with survivors of hate. They should also learn more about hate groups and their ideologies, so that their coverage is more informed and commensurate with the threat they pose. Otherwise, they will exacerbate the widespread misperception that hate and white supremacy are an isolated phenomena rather than an intensifying and growing one. In addition, they should invite advocates who document and fight hate to share their expertise. It's absurd to speculate about hate, when advocates work on these issues every day.

The media must also be more conscientious in how they describe the triple sins of mass shootings, hate violence, and terrorism. White suspects are typically humanized, described as struggling with mental health issues, and considered capable of rehabilitation. They are nearly always described as being driven by personal grievance rather than by a hateful ideology. Major news outlets called Dylann Roof, who killed nine people in a Charleston church in 2015, a "loner" and did not push back when politicians like Senator Lindsey Graham called him "one of these whacked-out kids."[63] Stephen Paddock, who was responsible for the deadliest mass shooting in modern U.S. history when he opened fire on a concert in Las Vegas in 2017, was described as a country music fan who lived a quiet life.[64] He too was called a "lone wolf," just like Roof.[65] But when the suspect is Muslim,

brown, black, or a combination thereof, they are described as evil
terrorists inspired by a hateful ideology and incapable of rehabilitation (the word "terrorist," in fact, is used to withhold rights
and dehumanize suspects, which is why the term should be abandoned altogether).[66] This dangerous double standard diminishes
the threat of ideologies like white supremacy, and national crises
like gun violence, and overstates the threat of foreign-inspired
violence. Hate is also seen as a series of separate occurrences
rather than as a manifestation of a deeper ideology, like white
supremacy, that we must condemn and reject. Many news outlets that covered the Portland stabbing that left two dead, for
example, failed to mention the murder of Richard W. Collins III,
a black student, by another white supremacist a few days earlier at the University of Maryland.[67] Research now shows that
attacks perpetrated by Muslims receive four and a half times
more media coverage than those perpetrated by non-Muslims.[68]

The media, of course, also exercises immense influence on
popular culture, and should be more inclusive and equitable in
their portrayals and representations of vulnerable communities.
Transgender, undocumented, and characters with disabilities, for
example, are often played by people from other communities, and
their characters are almost invariably essentialized. A recent study
found that 95 percent of characters with disabilities on television
are played by able-bodied actors.[69] In addition, diverse community members are not portrayed as everyday people striving to
make a difference and lead a better life; instead, their identity
forms the entire basis of their character. In the case of Muslims
and Arabs, it is worse. They are usually cast as criminals and terrorists.[70] Reductionist and negative portrayals reinforce false and
dangerous stereotypes about already vulnerable communities.

Silicon Valley and Technology Companies

In the wake of the Charlottesville protests, many technology
companies blocked and terminated users expressing hateful

ideologies, including white supremacy. Ever since, white supremacists have had difficulty accessing the shared economy through
applications like Uber and Airbnb; raising funds through Apple
Pay, PayPal, and other payment services; connecting to like-
minded hate mongers through social media platforms like Facebook and Twitter; and hosting and delivering content online
through Cloudflare, Google, and GoDaddy.[71] After Charlottesville, those three sites refused service and delisted the Daily
Stormer, the white supremacist blog that targeted Taylor Dumpson (chapter 2) and Tanya Gersh (chapter 8).[72] These companies
are not bound by the First Amendment, and under the law are
free to host or eliminate any content they wish.

Hate cannot be eradicated from the top down, only from the
bottom up, and yet this is still a welcome development. Technology companies should not facilitate the spread of white supremacy. It is true that some users and sites have moved to the dark web,
and have become self-professed free speech martyrs, which is in
itself a recruiting tool.[73] But the aggregate effect of being locked
out of the internet is immense. White supremacists will have
greater difficulty connecting, recruiting, and fundraising. Online
bullying and trolling will also hopefully dissipate, making more
room for diverse voices. As described in this book, many activists
have reduced their use of social media or abandoned it altogether
because of incessant abuse. At least one study has already found
that banning hate mongers works and can reduce hate across an
entire platform.[74] These interventions are particularly important
because of how difficult it is to litigate and prove the crime of
cyberstalking, commonly defined as repeated conduct that seeks
to cause emotional distress and fear of physical harm.[75]

But we must tread carefully. The decision to suspend an
account is often made by a human being or budding artificial
intelligence program that can be evaded and mistakes can happen.[76] Besides, the heroes of today can be the foes of tomorrow.
Technology companies may target white supremacists today,
but could go after Black Lives Matter activists next. Technol-

ogy companies must have meaningful checks in place, including allowing users to appeal decisions, better informed consent about user changes and policies, and far greater transparency with users and regulators.[77] We must know the criteria for banning users and how such criteria are applied.[78] Companies should be required to file annual reports detailing the number of banned users and their reasoning. This transparency is particularly critical given the dangerous repeal of net neutrality. Internet service providers now have the extraordinary power to censor online content in invisible and dangerous ways, and we must ensure that they remain committed to free speech, while meaningfully taking on hate.

Some will contend that giving companies this kind of power is dangerous. These institutions, after all, are unelected and undemocratic, driven by profit, and have previously caved to the will of state authorities.[79] These are legitimate and well-founded concerns. And yet, these companies have solved extraordinarily challenging problems, bridged communities, and continue to innovate. With time, they can cultivate a more equitable and safe space online. The internet is young and we are just beginning to understand how it affects our daily lives. Greater transparency and a robust conversation between companies, regulators, and users will allow us to develop stronger social norms for online engagement. We must also remember that those with the most to lose overwhelmingly favor companies taking on hate. Color of Change, the largest online racial justice advocacy organization, has long spearheaded these efforts, alongside countless community organizations.[80]

Schools and Universities

Schools and universities must do more to protect survivors and vulnerable communities on campus. In their report "After the Election, The Trump Effect," the Southern Policy Law Center found that 90 percent of polled educators believed that their school had been negatively affected by the election, and roughly 25 percent said they knew of fights, threats, assaults, and other incidents that could be traced directly to election rhetoric.[81] In their report, "Let Her Learn," the National Women's Law Center found that more than one in six girls ranging between the ages of fourteen and eighteen have been harassed since Trump's election.[82]

Some of the best ways to curb bullying in schools are found in this book. The needs of the student must control. Teachers, administrators, the family, and student must collaborate; focus on education and classroom presentations; concentrate on the place where the bullying is taking place; and reject zero-tolerance policies in favor of dialogue. Parents cannot be absolved, either. Students continue to be exempt from educational and interfaith presentations because their parents claim that schools are "religion-free zones." Yet sometimes it is these same students who continue to bully others.

Bullying is not a rite of passage. Students have the right to be free from harassment in school, just as adults do in the workplace. In addition, bullying, left untreated, can morph into something much worse. Time-tested preventive measures include providing anti-bullying training to school staff; scrupulously monitoring hot spots including playgrounds and, increasingly, the internet; preemptively delivering diversity, equity, and inclusion presentations in class and across the school; and ensuring that staff and communities have easy and ready access to anti-bullying materials.[83]

Universities too must center survivors and their communities when responding to hate. They must heed the warning signs, and when hate strikes, they should be guided by the needs of students, rather than brushing it aside or co-opting it for political gain. They should create rapid-response teams, which can curb, track, and respond to hate incidents on campus—a recommendation that has been made by educators nationwide.[84] In response to activism and student demands after the murder of

Richard Collins III, the University of Maryland formed a rapid-response team, increased their budget for diversity and inclusion, hired a hate-bias-response coordinator, and agreed to annually report the number of hate bias incidents on campus.[85] All students should be treated equally and fairly. Students deserve to be free from harm on campus regardless of their political beliefs, including support of the Palestinian-led Boycott, Divestment, and Sanctions movement.

Schools and universities must also cultivate difficult conversations on race, faith, immigration, gender, sexuality, and the like on campus. They must be attentive to the collective trauma of marginalized communities, in particular black and Native students who have to go about their everyday lives despite recurring incidents of hate and political brutality. Students must have the resources they need to heal and move forward, including safe spaces to gather and meet, funding for programming, and sufficient mental health resources and counseling services offered by professionals from their communities. This is especially true for universities that champion free speech above all else. Even lawful forms of hate can affect a student's ability to learn, grow, and thrive.[86]

Finally, universities must protect survivors of sexual assault and gender violence on campus by rigorously enforcing Title IX. Despite new guidelines by the Department of Education, universities are still afforded considerable latitude in how they address Title IX complaints and can still follow the Obama-era guidance.[87] Schools must not roll back survivors' rights and must ensure that survivors receive proper support and resources, including health care and tutoring. All students should be able to live healthily, happily, and free from abuse.

White Allies and Empathy

Our white allies must step up as well. They must tackle the racism, white anxiety, sexism, and economic deprivation that culminated in Trump's rise to power. It is not enough for marginalized communities to host interfaith and interracial conversations: white America must confront white supremacy and racism. They must root it out town by town and city by city, just like the cancer it is. Racism comes in many forms. It is not just taking to the streets of Charlottesville and spouting hate for the world to see. It is also leaving the neighborhood when a diverse family moves next door. It is pulling children from school because immigrant children want to be their friends. It is opposing the construction of a mosque because "their" beliefs do not belong in "this town." It is the microaggressions and invisible othering, where some get sympathy and understanding, but others get disdain and intolerance.

A majority of white Americans feel they are victims of discrimination, despite their many immense privileges.[88] These Americans have to unpack their own anxiety, and understand that the projects of justice and equity are not assaults on their racial identity. They are about collective liberation, and making the world a better place for us all. They must understand that their waning demographic and economic power is not the result of discrimination; it is a more level playing field. And those who voted for Trump must realize that though they may not be racists, they are at least bystanders to racism. Their tacit acceptance made his overt racism possible. Our young children—who are bullied on the playground, punched on the street, and sometimes forced to abandon their identity—do not distinguish between racists and bystanders to racism. Nor should you. The incorrigible political correctness that has become a hallmark of our lives must be replaced with an unwavering commitment to dialogue, truth, and accountability.

Still, it is nevertheless true that many white Americans have experienced economic deprivation, just like vulnerable communities, including people of color. The gulf between city and hinterland feels insurmountable, and the disparity between the haves and have-nots seems irreconcilable. It often feels like there are two economies in this country, and the majority of Americans have been locked out. But we can overcome it together because we have overcome so much worse in our history. We aspire to a world of equity, justice, and inclusion, where we all have a seat at the table. We long for a nation that brims with light for all our children to see.

Many of us will meet you halfway. There is no moral equivalence between racism and inclusion, or misogyny and equality, but we are still capable of radical empathy. I know of no better example than that of the Sikhs of Oak Creek, Wisconsin. On August 6, 2012, a white supremacist stormed a Sikh gurdwara, killing six and injuring several others, before taking his own life. It was one of the deadliest hate crimes and mass shootings at a house of worship in American history. When the Sikh community later gathered, they recited their holy prayer, the *ardaas*, and mourned those they lost. But they also prayed for the soul of the shooter.[89] Even in the wake of atrocity, they were committed to a better tomorrow.

Resilience and Reconciliation

Despite it all, survivors and communities remain resilient and optimistic, and are finding ways to resist. We have seen that they are debunking hateful myths about refugees and extreme vetting; building more inclusive communities on college campuses; securing stronger protections for crime victims; organizing a community defense to mass deportation; fighting for gender violence survivors; passing police accountability measures; educating others about Muslims and Arabs; taking on organized white supremacy; proactively combating bullying; building community with the families of people who have stood up to hate; telling the stories of trans persons and people with disabilities; fighting for the rights of vulnerable students at universities; and advocating for the sovereignty and dignity of Native communities.

The most vulnerable among us are not retreating or

abandoning hope. They are educating, organizing, and advocating. They are on the front lines combating hate, and coming together in neighborhoods, schools, workplaces, and community centers. So many survivors are willing to reconcile and talk, even in the wake of unimaginable grief. They want accountability, not retribution. They are living and practicing restorative justice in the most carceral state in modern history.

In this book alone, they rejected zero-tolerance policies in the classroom, choosing education and empathy instead. They responded to hateful messages because they believe that even their most virulent critics can change. After a hate crime, some did not call the police; they forged a community defense and cultivated dialogue instead. They recommended in open court and elsewhere that assailants learn about their communities rather than languish in jail. Even in the wake of murder, they talked about the importance of community, lamenting that some in this world never have one.

Their commitment to racial, social, and economic justice will remain steadfast, as must ours. We will build a united front in and across our diverse communities. The coalitions of tomorrow will be deeper and stronger than those of today. We will forge a collective defense against hate and criminalization, where our diverse communities can find comfort and joy. We will teach our children to survive and thrive, even when others push them down. We will teach them to rise, just as we did, and remind them of what our ancestors endured long before us. We will teach them to forgive and reconcile, because empathy and tenderness are innate to who we are. We will build community and thrive. We will press on, just like we have always done.

ACKNOWLEDGMENTS

This book required a community. So many people connected me to survivors, offered me a place to stay, and drove me around on unfamiliar roads in unfamiliar places. Community activists and organizations do this work every day, opened doors for me, and shared their dreams and aspirations with me. This is their book, too.

I could not have completed this project without my mom's enduring love and endless supply of chai. Gobind, Ravneet, my dad, Sahib, and little Nankee helped along the way, as did my family's two black German shepherds, Jake and Sophie. If only human beings could love the way they do.

Ziad Abu-Rish, Noura Erakat, Maher Bitar, Nadia Aziz, and Paloma Falcon listened, questioned, and gently pushed. Rajiv Nunna, Vijay Das, and Sukhman Dhami made me laugh, when sometimes that was what I needed most. Ola Wazwaz and Lena Ghannam kept me optimistic and grateful, a spirit that I hope animates this book. Nancy Okail, Laila Jadallah, and Hesham Sallam were always there.

Deepa Iyer gave her heart and soul to this project. She read drafts and grounded me in community. She was a constant source of inspiration and hope.

My students at Georgetown and Vanderbilt offered wise counsel, as did the young students at the United World College in New Mexico, which generously supported this book through a fellowship in residence. I am also grateful to Shireen Zaman with the Proteus Fund for her vision and support of my work, even when it has taken an unconventional route.

The New Press and Writers House were superb. Ben Woodward was patient and open-minded, and Susan Ginsburg was always thinking ahead. Namrata Tripathi, a lifelong friend and editor, was a wonderful resource from the beginning.

Special thanks also to Imraan Siddiqi, Seth Pritchett, Isis Misdary, Mandeep Manku, Lakshmi Sridaran, Fatima Goss Graves, Almas Sayeed, Joseph Santos-Lyons, Dyjuana Hudson, Anna Duncan, Catalina Nieto, Christopher Petrella, Akiesha Anderson, Zakir Khan, Seemab Hussaini, Rebecca Sturtevant, David Dinielli, Naomi Swinton, Linda Sarsour, Nadia Firozvi, Abed Ayoub, Dyne Suh, Marian Mikhail, Maya Berry, Kymberlie Quong Charles, Kenne Dibner, Nate McCray, Dena Takruri, Alice Wong, Amanda McCloskey, Janeen Comenote, Chahta Summer, Karin Wang, Emily Waters, Ranjit Singh, Mike Greiner, Srini Bhagavan, and the PCU, all of whom supported this project.

Over the years there have been those who have instilled in me a love for words. This affection has little to do with advocacy or persuasion. It is about art and the beauty of writing. It is about seeking shelter in words when you cannot find it elsewhere. I am grateful to everyone who has fostered and nurtured this love. You know who you are.

> In his text, the writer sets up house. Just as he
> trundles papers, books, pencils, documents untidily

from room to room, he creates the same disorder in his thoughts. They become pieces of furniture that he sinks into, content or irritable. He strokes them affectionately, wears them out, mixes them up, re-arranges, ruins them. For a man who no longer has a homeland, writing becomes a place to live.

—Theodor Adorno, *Minima Moralia: Reflections from a Damaged Life*

NOTES

Introduction: American Hate

1. For additional information about the Bellingham riots, see David Cahn, "The 1907 Bellingham Riots in Historical Context," Seattle Civil Rights and Labor History Project, depts.washington.edu/civilr/bham_history.htm.

2. Many lists have been compiled detailing these incidents. See, e.g., Mehdi Hasan, "Donald Trump Has Been a Racist All His Life—And He Isn't Going to Change After Charlottesville," *The Intercept*, August 15, 2017, theintercept.com/2017/08/15/donald-trump-has bee n-a-racist-all-his-life-and-he-isnt-going-to-change-after-charlottesville; Lydia O'Connor and Daniel Marans, "Trump Condemned Racism as 'Evil.' Here Are 20 Times He Embraced It," *Huffington Post*, August 14, 2017, www.huffingtonpost.com/entry/trump-racism -examples_us_5991dcabe4b09071f69b9261; Lisa Desjardins, "Every Moment in Trump's Charged Relationship with Race," *PBS News-Hour*, August 22, 2017, www.pbs.org/newshour/politics/every-moment -donald-trumps-long-complicated-history-race.

3. Lucia Graves and Sam Morris, "The Trump Allegations," *The Guardian*, November 29, 2017.

4. See, e.g., note 2.

5. Rebecca Hersher and Carrie Johnson, "Trump Administration Rescinds Obama Rule on Transgender Students' Bathroom Use," *The Two-Way* (NPR), February 22, 2017, www.npr.org/sections/thetwo-way/2017/02/22/516664633/trump-administration-rescinds-obama-rule-on-transgender-students-bathroom-use; Mary Kay Mallonee and Eli Watkins, "DOJ Scaling Back Program to Reform Police Departments," *CNN*, September 15, 2017, www.cnn.com/2017/09/15/politics/doj-police-program/index.html.

6. Jen Kirby, "Trump Wants Fewer Immigrants from 'Shithole Countries' and More from Places Like Norway," *Vox*, January 11, 2018, www.vox.com/2018/1/11/16880750/trump-immigrants-shithole-countries-norway.

7. Amber Phillips, "That Time the Senate Denied Jeff Sessions a Federal Judgeship over Accusations of Racism," *Washington Post*, January 10, 2017.

8. Peter Beinart, "Mike Pompeo at State Would Enable Trump's Worst Instincts," *The Atlantic*, November 30, 2017.

9. Matt Broomfield, "Nazi-linked Group 'Proud' That Top Donald Trump Aide Wore Its Medal," *The Independent*, April 8, 2017; Spencer Ackerman, "FBI Fired Sebastian Gorka for Anti-Muslim Diatribes," *Daily Beast*, June 21, 2017, www.thedailybeast.com/fbi-fired-sebastian-gorka-for-anti-muslim-diatribes.

10. Andrew Kaczynski and Chris Massie, "In College, Trump Aide Stephen Miller Led Controversial 'Terrorism Awareness Project,'" *CNN*, February 15, 2017, www.cnn.com/2017/02/15/politics/kfile-stephen-miller-terrorism-awareness/index.html.

11. Asawin Suebsaeng, "Trump's Chief Strategist Steve Bannon: 'I'm a Nationalist,' Totally Not Racist!," *Daily Beast*, November 18, 2016, www.thedailybeast.com/trumps-chief-strategist-steve-bannon-im-a-nationalist-totally-not-racist.

12. Southern Poverty Law Center, "The Trump Effect: The Impact of the 2016 Presidential Election on our Nation's Schools," November 28, 2016, www.splcenter.org/20161128/trump-effect-impact-2016-presidential-election-our-nations-schools#pdf.

13. National Women's Law Center, "Let Her Learn," April 2017, https://nwlc-ciw49tixgw5lbab.stackpathdns.com/wp-content/uploads/2017/04/final_nwlc_Gates_HarassmentViolence.pdf.

14. Chandelis R. Duster, "With Rise in Racially Charged Incidents on Campus, Colleges Work to Ease Students' Fears," *NBC News*, October 1, 2017, www.nbcnews.com/news/nbcblk/rise-racially-charged-incidents-campus-colleges-work-ease-students-fears-n806241.

15. Nancy Coleman, "On Average, 9 Mosques Have Been Targeted Every Month This Year," *CNN*, August 7, 2017, www.cnn.com/2017/03/20/us/mosques-targeted-2017-trnd/index.html.

16. Joe Heim, "Recounting a Day of Rage, Hate, Violence and Death," *Washington Post*, August 14, 2017, www.washingtonpost.com/graphics/2017/local/charlottesville-timeline/.

17. Christopher Mathias, "The Killing of Khalid Jabara Is an American Tragedy," *Huffington Post*, August 23, 2016, www.huffingtonpost.com/entry/khalid-jabara-killed_us_57b493b8e4b0b42c38afb448.

18. Mark Berman and Samantha Schmidt, "He Yelled 'Get Out of My Country,' Witnesses Say, and Then Shot 2 Men from India, Killing One," *Washington Post*, February 27, 2017.

19. Jamiles Lartey, "White Veteran 'Regarded Fatal Stabbing of Black Man as Practice for Larger Attack,'" *The Guardian*, March 24, 2017.

20. Dave Zirin, "A Lynching on the University of Maryland Campus," *The Nation*, May 22, 2017, www.thenation.com/article/lynching-university-maryland-campus.

21. Tom Porter, "Man Arrested for Oregon Stabbings Was 'Known White Supremacist,'" *Newsweek*, May 28, 2017, www.newsweek.com/portland-oregon-jeremy-christian-616927.

22. Emily Shugerman, "Nabra Hassanen's Father Says She Was '100%' Killed for Being Muslim," *The Independent*, June 19, 2017.

23. "These Are the Trans People Killed in 2017," *The Advocate*, www.advocate.com/transgender/2017/12/14/these-are-trans-people-killed-2017

24. See, e.g., Introduction note 2.

25. See, e.g., Introduction note 5.

26. FBI Uniform Crime Reporting, 2016 Hate Crime Statistics, ucr.fbi.gov/hate-crime/2016/tables/table-1; U.S. Department of Justice, Bureau of Justice Statistics, Hate Crime Victimization, 2004-2015 June 2017, www.bjs.gov/content/pub/pdf/hcv0415.pdf.

27. See, e.g., South Asian Americans Leading Together, "Power, Pain, Potential," saalt.org/wp-content/uploads/2017/01/SAALT_Power_rpt_final3_lorez.pdf; Council on American Islamic Relations, *Civil Rights Report 2017*, cairky.com/images/documents/2017%20Empowerment%20of%20Fear.pdf; Anti-Defamation League, "ADL Audit: US Anti-Semitic Incidents Surged in 2016-17," www.adl.org/sites/default/files/documents/Anti-Semitic%20Audit%20Print_vf2.pdf; Muslim Advocates, "Map: Recent Incidents of Anti-Muslim Hate Crimes," www.muslimadvocates.org/map-anti-muslim-hate-crimes.

28. Southern Poverty Law Center, Hatewatch, December 16, 2016, www.splcenter.org/hatewatch/2016/12/16/update-1094-bias-related -incidents-month-following-election.

29. Tess Owen, "Anti Muslim Hate Is on the Rise," *Vice News*, November 14, 2017, news.vice.com/en_us/article/d3xxj7/anti-muslim-hate-c rimes-skyrocketed-again-in-2016-fbi-data-says; Sam Petulla, Tammy Kupperman, and Jessica Schneider, "The Number of Hate Crimes Rose in 2016," *CNN*, November 13, 2017, www.cnn.com/2017/11/13/politics /hate-crimes-fbi-2016-rise/index.html.

2: Taylor Dumpson

1. Anti-Defamation League, "White Supremacist Propaganda Surges on Campus," January 29, 2018, www.adl.org/education/resources /reports/white-supremacist-propaganda-surges-on-campus.

5: Alexandra Brodsky

1. Erica L. Green and Sheryl Gay Stolberg, "Campus Rape Policies Get a New Look as the Accused Get DeVos's Ear," *New York Times*, July 12, 2017.

7: Marwan Kreidie and Shahid Hashmi

1. Jenna Johnson, "Trump Calls for 'Total and Complete Shutdown of Muslims Entering the United States,'" *Washington Post*, December 7, 2015.

8: Tanya Gersh

1. Daniel Lombroso and Yoni Appelbaum, "'Hail Trump!': White Nationalists Salute the President-Elect," *The Atlantic*, November 21, 2016.

2. Southern Poverty Law Center, "Andrew Anglin," "https://www .splcenter.org/fighting-hate/extremist-files/individual/andrew-anglin.

3. *Tanya Gersh v. Andrew Anglin*, Complaint, United States District Court, District of Montana, Missoula Division, April 18, 2017, https:// www.splcenter.org/sites/default/files/whitefish_complaint_finalstamped .pdf.

9: Harjit Kaur

1. Department of Health and Human Services, "What Is Bullying," StopBullying.Gov, www.stopbullying.gov/what-is-bullying/index.html.

2. Rediff, "Sodhi Murder Trial Begins," September 4, 2003, www .rediff.com/us/2003/sep/03sodhi.htm.

Conclusion: Hope in a Time of Despair

1. Kelli Craig-Henderson and Lloyd Sloan, "After the Hate: Helping Psychologists Help Victims of Racist Hate Crime," *Clinical Psychology: Science and Practice* 10 (2006): 481–490, 10.1093/clipsy.bpg048 citing G.M. Herek, J.R. Gillis, J.C. Cogan, & E.K. Glunt, "Hate Crime Victimization Among Lesbian, Gay, and Bisexual Adults: Prevalence, Psychological Correlates and Methodological Issues," *Journal of Interpersonal Violence*, 12 (1997), 195–215.

2. Ibid.

3. Monique Noelle, "The Ripple Effect of a Sexual Orientation Hate Crime: The Psychological Impact of the Murder of Matthew Shepard on Non-Heterosexual People," (master's thesis, 2000), Masters Theses 1911–February 2014, 2354, scholarworks.umass.edu/theses/2354; American Psychological Association, The Psychology of Hate Crimes, www.apa.org/advocacy/civil-rights/hate-crimes.pdf.

4. Douglas Jacobs, "We're Sick of Racism, Literally," *New York Times*, November 11, 2017, www.nytimes.com/2017/11/11/opinion /sunday/sick-of-racism-literally.html.

5. Nina Martin and Renee Montagne, "Nothing Protects Black Women from Dying in Pregnancy and Childbirth," *ProPublica*, December 7, 2017, www.propublica.org/article/nothing-protects-black-women-from -dying-in-pregnancy-and-childbirth.

6. Ibid.

7. Ellen Garrison, " 'Let's Fix It.' Hundreds Attend Elk Grove Town Hall After Hate Note Targets Black Salon," *Sacramento Bee*, October 24, 2017, www.sacbee.com/news/local/article180687036.html; Elk Grove News, "Town Hall Meeting on Elk Grove Relations Part Catharsis, Part Healing," October 24, 2017, www.elkgrovenews.net/2017/10 /town-hall-meeting-on-elk-grove-race.html.

8. Gray Hall and Jeff Chirico, "Racist Graffiti Found on Bucks County School," *ABC Action News*, August 24, 2017, 6abc.com/racist -graffiti-found-on-bucks-county-school/2338308.

9. Karen Sakata, "How Schools Deal with Discrimination and Hate Speech," *Mercury News*, December 21, 2017, www.mercurynews.com /2017/12/21/opinion-how-schools-deal-with-discrimination-and-hate -speech.

10. Noa Yadidi, "DOJ Report: Majority of Hate Crimes Go Unreported," *CNN*, June 29, 2017, www.cnn.com/2017/06/29/politics/doj-hate -crime-report/index.html.

11. See, e.g., Ken Schwencke, "Confusion, Fear, Cynicism: Why People Don't Report Hate Incidents," *ProPublica*, July 31, 2017, www.propublica.org/article/confusion-fear-cynicism-why-people-dont -report-hate-incidents.

12. A Call to Action by Jay Hirabayashi, Holly Yasui, and Karen Korematsu, Stop Repeating History!, stoprepeatinghistory.org.

13. Sam Levin, "Over My Dead Body: Tribe Aims to Block Trump's Border Wall on Arizona Land," *The Guardian*, January 26, 2017.

14. United We Dream, "Immigrant Youth and Allies Mobilize to Defend DACA & TPS in Cities and States Across the Country," August 15, 2017, unitedwedream.org/2017/08/immigrant-youth-and-allies-mob ilize-to-defend-daca-tps-in-cities-and-states-across-the-country.

15. See, e.g., Alicia Garza, "A Herstory of the #BlackLivesMatter Movement," *Feminist Wire*, October 7, 2014, www.thefeministwire .com/2014/10/blacklivesmatter-2.

16. Letters for Black Lives, "Dear Mom, Dad, Uncle, Auntie: Black Lives Matter to Us, Too," *Medium*, July 11, 2016, lettersforblacklives.com /dear-mom-dad-uncle-auntie-black-lives-matter-to-us-too-7ca577 d59f4c.

17. Emma Whitford, "Brooklyn Neighborhood Establishes 'Hate Free Zone' in Wake of Trump Executive Orders," *The Gothamist*, January 26, 2017, gothamist.com/2017/01/26/hate_free_zone_brooklyn.php.

18. Gabriella Borter, "More Churches Are Offering Sanctuary for Immigrants Under Trump," *Huffington Post*, August 1, 2017, www.huffingtonpost .com/entry/trump-sanctuary-churches_us_5980e03ce4b09d24e993a167; Sarah Ruiz Grossman, "Why This Church Is Providing 'Sanctuary' to Undocumented Immigrants," *Huffington Post*, October 20, 2017, www.huffingtonpost.com/entry/southside-presbyterian-church-sanctuary -movement_us_59b722dfe4b027c149e1be39.

19. Issie Lapowsky, "A Portable Panic Button for Immigrants Swept Up In Raids," *Wired*, March 10, 2017.

20. Minyoung Park, "5 Must-Have Apps for Undocumented Immigrants," CNN, March 30, 2017.

21. Rhana Natour, "Sights Set on 2018, the Women's March Is Throwing a Convention," *PBS NewsHour*, September 27, 2017, www .pbs.org/newshour/politics/sights-set-2018-womens-march-throwing -convention.

22. LA Kauffman, "The Resistance to Trump Is Blossoming—and Building a Movement to Last," *The Guardian*, November 9, 2017.

23. See, e.g., Communities Against Hate, communitiesagainsthate. org/about.

24. See, e.g., NoMuslimBanEver, www.nomuslimbanever.com.

25. Courtney Terlicki, "Hate Groups, Free Speech Discussed at Wausau Town Hall," WKOW.com, September 13, 2017, www.wkow.com/ story/36359747/2017/09/Wednesday/hate-groups-free-speech-to-be -discussed-at-wausau-town-hall.

26. See also Lawyer's Committee for Civil Rights Under Law, "Community Response Toolkit: When Hate Groups Come to Town," 8449nohate.org/wp-content/uploads/2017/06/Community-Response -Toolkit.HateGroups.pdf.

27. Southern Poverty Law Center, "Ten Ways to Fight Hate: A Community Response Guide," August 14, 2017, www.splcenter.org/20170814 /ten-ways-fight-hate-community-response-guide.

28. "Black Lives Matter Organizers Won't Take Part in Counterprotests," *Daily News Journal*, October 27, 2017, www.dnj.com/story /news/local/2017/10/27/black-lives-matter-organizers-wont-take-part -counter-protests/808375001.

29. See, e.g., Deepa Iyer, "Reckoning With Trauma Sixteen Years After," *Medium*, September 10, 2017, medium.com/@dviyer/https -medium-com-dviyer-reckoning-with-trauma-16-years-after-sept11 -98e063b6197e.

30. National Church Arson Task Force, "National Church Arson Task Force Issues Fourth Report: Number of Arsons at America's Houses of Worship Continues to Decline," news release, September 15, 2000, www.justice.gov/opa/pr/2000/September/542cr.htm.

31. Ibid.

32. Community organizations have made this request during prior administrations as well. See, e.g., *Hate Crimes and the Threat of Domestic Extremism Hearing, Senate Committee on the Judiciary Subcommittee on the Constitution, Civil Rights, and Human Rights*, September 9, 2012 (written statement of Deepa Iyer), saalt.org/wp -content/uploads/2012/09/SAALT-Statement-of-the-Record.pdf.

33. Arjun Sethi, "Attacks Like Portland's Will Keep Happening Unless We All Fight White Supremacy," *Washington Post*, May 29, 2017.

34. See, e.g., The Bureau of Investigative Journalism, "Drone Warfare," www.thebureauinvestigates.com/projects/drone-war; Baher Azmy, "Closing Time," *Slate*, January 11, 2018, slate.com/news-and -politics/2018/01/trumps-anti-muslim-bigotry-clarifies-guantanamo -bays-awfulness.html; Naomi Klein and Opal Tometi, "Forget *Coates v. West*—We All Have a Duty to Confront the Full Reach of U.S. Empire," *The Intercept*, December 21, 2017, theintercept.com/2017/12/21/cornel -west-ta-nehisi-coates-feud.

35. Martin Luther King Jr., "Beyond Vietnam: A Time to Break Silence," www.youtube.com/watch?v=3Qf6x9_MLD0.

36. See, e.g., Introduction note 2; Nicholas Fandos, "Trump's View of Syria: How It Evolved, in 19 Tweets," *New York Times*, April 7, 2017.

37. Jesselyn Cook, "7 Lies Donald Trump Has Spread About Syrian Refugees Entering the U.S.," *Huffington Post*, October 25, 2016, www.huffingtonpost.com/entry/donald-trump-refugee-crisis_us_ 5807809ae4b0180a36e7ac14.

38. Jenna Johnson and Abigail Hauslohner, " 'I Think Islam Hates Us': A Timeline of Trump's Comments About Islam and Muslims," *Washington Post*, May 20, 2017.

39. Christopher Cadelago and Anita Chabria, "Defying Trump Again, Jerry Brown Pardons Immigrants About to Be Deported," *Sacramento Bee*, December 23, 2017, www.sacbee.com/news/politics-government /capitol-alert/article191430714.html.

40. Yara Simon, "28 Universities That Vow to Offer Sanctuary to Their Undocumented Students," *Remezcla*, November 22, 2016, remezcla.com /lists/culture/sanctuary-campus-daca.

41. Mythili Sampathkumar, "Majority of Terrorists Who Have Attacked America Are Not Muslim, New Study Finds," *The Independent*, June 23, 2017; Uri Friedman, "Where America's Terrorists Actually Come From," *The Atlantic*, January 30, 2017.

42. Southern Poverty Law Center, "Hate Groups Increase for Second Consecutive Year as Trump Electrifies Radical Right," February 15, 2017, www.splcenter.org/news/2017/02/15/hate-groups-increase-second -consecutive-year-trump-electrifies-radical-right.

43. Jana Winter, "FBI and DHS Warned of Growing Threat from White Supremacists Months Ago," *Foreign Policy*, August 14, 2017, foreignpolicy.com/2017/08/14/fbi-and-dhs-warned-of-growing-threat -from-white-supremacists-months-ago.

44. H.R. 2899, Countering Violent Extremism Act of 2015, Coalition Letter to Reps. Michael McCaul and Bennie G. Thompson, July 15, 2015, www.brennancenter.org/sites/default/files/analysis/071015%20 Letter%20to%20H.%20Comm%20on%20Homeland%20Sec.%20Re .%20HR%202899%20%20.pdf.

45. Ibid.

46. Expansion of Countering Violent Extremism Programs, Coalition Letter to Reps. Kevin McCarthy, Mitch McConnell, Nancy Pelosi, and Chuck Schumer, September 7, 2017, www.brennancenter.org/sites /default/files/analysis/9.7.17%20CVE%20Letter%20FINAL.pdf.

47. Khaled Beydoun and Justin Hansford, "The FBI's Dangerous Crackdown on 'Black Identity Extremists,'" *New York Times*, November 15, 2017.

48. Anti-Defamation League, "Hate Crime Laws," 2012, www.adl.org /sites/default/files/documents/assets/pdf/combating-hate/Hate-Crimes -Law.pdf.

49. Joshua Rhett Miller, "Airbnb Host Fined, Ordered to Take College Course After Turning Away Asian Guest," *New York Post*, July 13, 2017, nypost.com/2017/07/13/airbnb-host-fined-ordered-to -take-college-course-for-turning-away-asian-guest.

50. A.C. Thompson and Patrick G. Lee, "Claims of 'Homosexual Agenda' Help Kill Hate Crimes Laws in 5 States," *ProPublica*, February 6, 2017, www.propublica.org/article/claims-of-homosexual-agenda -help-kill-hate-crimes-laws-in-five-states.

51. Ann E. Marimow and Rachel Weiner, "Hateful Acts May Be Rising, But Will Court Cases Follow?," *Washington Post*, March 25, 2017.

52. Jonathan H. Adler, "Sixth Circuit Reverses Amish Beard-Cutting Hate Crime Convictions," *Washington Post*, September 1, 2014.

53. See, e.g., Arjun Sethi, "Hate-Crime Laws Aren't Strong Enough," *USA Today*, August 23, 2016, www.usatoday.com/story/opinion/2016 /08/23/hate-crimes-violence-muslims-arab-americans-islamophobia -sikhs-transgender-column/89101382; Marty Lederman, "Disturbing Reversal of Hate-Crime Convictions in Amish Hair-Cutting Case," *Balkinization*, August 28, 2014, balkin.blogspot.com/2014/08/disturbing -reversal-of-hate-crime.html.

54. Terrence McCoy, "Chapel Hill Killings: Why Hate Crimes Are So Hard to Prove," *Washington Post*, February 12, 2015.

55. Christina A. Cassidy, "Patchy Reporting Undercuts National Hate Crimes Count," Associated Press, June 5, 2016, apnews.com /8247a1d2f76b4baea2a121186dedf768/ap-patchy-reporting -undercuts-national-hate-crimes-count.

56. Ken Schwencke, "Why America Fails at Gathering Hate Crime Statistics," *ProPublica*, December 4, 2017, www.propublica.org/article /why-america-fails-at-gathering-hate-crime-statistics.

57. A.C. Thompson, Rohan Naik, and Ken Schwencke, "Hate Crime Training for Police Is Often Inadequate, Sometimes Nonexistent," *ProPublica*, November 29, 2017, www.propublica.org/article/hate-crime -training-for-police-is-often-inadequate-sometimes-nonexistent.

58. Ibid.

59. Chris Fuchs, "Advocates Warn of Possible Underreporting in FBI Hate Crime Data," *NBC News*, December 18, 2017, www.nbcnews .com/news/asian-america/advocates-warn-possible-underreporting-fbi -hate-crime-data-n830711.

60. Kristin Garrity Sekerci, "Does Islamophobia Impact the Underreporting of FBI Hate Crime Data?," The Bridge Initiative at Georgetown University, bridge.georgetown.edu/islamophobia-impact-underreporting -fbi-hate-crime-data.

61. *ProPublica*, "Documenting Hate," projects.propublica.org/graphics /hatecrimes.

62. Jina Moore, "Reporting on Trauma: Rules and Responsibilities," Pulitzer Center, March 9, 2012, pulitzercenter.org/reporting /reporting-trauma-rules-and-responsibilities.

63. Anthea Butler, "Shooters of Color Are Called 'Terrorists' and 'Thugs.' Why Are White Shooters Called 'Mentally Ill?,'" *Washington Post*, June 18, 2015.

64. William Wan and Aaron C. Davis, "Las Vegas Gunman Stephen Paddock Enjoyed Gambling, Country Music; Lived Quiet Life Before Massacre," *Washington Post*, October 2, 2017, www.washingtonpost.com/news/post-nation/wp/2017/10/02/las-vegas-gunman-liked-to-gamble-listened-to-country-music-lived-quiet-retired-life-before-massacre. Note that the *Post* seems to have changed the headline, but the original is preserved in both the URL and in the article as reprinted on other news sites such as www.philly.com/philly/news/nation_world/las-vegas-gunman-stephen-paddock-enjoyed-gambling-country-music-lived-quiet-life-before-massacre-20171002.html.

65. John Bacon and Mike James, "Las Vegas Shooting: At Least 59 Dead, Gunman Was 'Crazed Lunatic Full of Hate,'" *USA Today*, October 2, 2017, www.usatoday.com/story/news/nation/2017/10/02/las-vegas-shooting/722191001.

66. Ramzi Kassem, "'Terrorism': A Word We Need to Retire," *New York Daily News*, November 8, 2017, www.nydailynews.com/opinion/terrorism-word-retire-article-1.3619971.

67. Sarah Ruiz-Grossman, "5 Things the Media Gets Wrong About White Supremacist Hate," *Huffington Post*, June 9, 2017, www.huffingtonpost.com/entry/media-white-supremacist-hate_us_593850d5e4b0b13f2c66667a.

68. Erin M. Kearns, Allison Betus, and Anthony Lemieux, "Yes, the Media Do Underreport Some Terrorists Attacks, Just Not the Ones Most People Think Of," *Washington Post*, March 13, 2017.

69. Elizabeth Wagmeister, "Able-Bodied Actors Play 95% of Disabled Characters in Top 10 TV Shows, Says New Study," *Variety*, July 13, 2016, variety.com/2016/tv/news/disabled-actors-television-study-1201813686.

70. Dave Schilling, "Bloodthirsty Terrorists and Duplicitous Spies: Does TV Have a Muslim Problem?," *The Guardian*, February 4, 2016.

71. Keith Collins, "A Running List of Websites and Apps That Have Banned, Blocked, Deleted, and Otherwise Dropped White Supremacists," *Quartz*, August 6, 2017, qz.com/1055141/what-websites-and-apps-have-banned-neo-nazis-and-white-supremacist.

72. Ibid.

73. Matthew Ingram, "Here's Why Twitter Banning 'Alt-Right' Accounts Is a Risky Strategy," *Fortune*, November 16, 2016, fortune.com/2016/11/16/twitter-ban-alt-right.

74. Tom McKay, "Study Finds Banning Reddit's Bigoted Jerkwards Worked," *Gizmodo*, September 11, 2017, gizmodo.com/study-finds-banning-reddits-bigoted-jerkwards-worked-1803766754.

75. Marlisse Silver Sweeney, "What the Law Can (and Can't) Do About Online Harassment," *The Atlantic*, November 12, 2014.

76. See, e.g., Julia Angwin and Hannes Grassegger, "Facebook's Secret Censorship Rules Protect White Men from Hate Speech But Not Black Children," *ProPublica*, June 28, 2017, www.propublica.org/article /facebook-hate-speech-censorship-internal-documents-algorithms; Yair Rosenberg, "Confessions of a Digital Nazi Hunter," *New York Times*, December 27, 2017, www.nytimes.com/2017/12/27/opinion/digital-nazi -hunter-trump.html.

77. Jillian York, "The Internet's 'Nazi Purge' Shows Who Really Controls Our Online Speech," *BuzzFeed News*, August 21, 2017, www .buzzfeed.com/jillianyork/silicon-valleys-nazi-purge.

78. OnlineCensorship.org is doing critical work in this area: onlinecensorship.org.

79. See, e.g., Stephen L. Carter, "The Problem with Banning White Supremacists from the Internet," *Chicago Tribune*, August 18, 2017, www.chicagotribune.com/news/opinion/commentary/ct-perspec-tech -daily-stormer-libertarian-0821-20170818-story.html; Glenn Greenwald, "Facebook Says It Is Deleting Accounts at the Direction of the U.S. and Israeli Governments," *The Intercept*, December 30, 2017, theintercept.com/2017/12/30/facebook-says-it-is-deleting-accounts -at-the-direction-of-the-u-s-and-israeli-governments.

80. Ruth Umoh, "How Companies Like Google and Facebook Are Standing Up to Neo-Nazis and Other Hate Groups," *CNBC*, August 16, 2017, www.cnbc.com/2017/08/16/google-and-facebook-are-standing -up-to-neo-nazis-and-other-hate-groups.html.

81. See Introduction note 12.

82. See Introduction note 13.

83. See, e.g., "How to Prevent Bullying," Stopbullying.gov, www .stopbullying.gov/prevention/index.html.

84. See, e.g., Shetal Vohra-Gupta and Naomi Reed, "More Universities Need Anti-Hate Policies," *University of Texas: Texas Perspectives*, August 31, 2017, news.utexas.edu/2017/08/31/more-universities-need -anti-hate-policies.

85. Jack Pointer, "University of Maryland President Announces Anti-Hate Action Plan," WTOP, May 25, 2017, https://wtop.com/education /2017/05/maryland-president-anti-hate-plan; Sarah Brown, "Why the U. of Maryland Is Hiring a 'Hate-Bias Response Coordinator,'" *Chronicle of Higher Education*, November 28, 2017, www.chronicle.com/article /Why-the-U-of-Maryland-Is/241904.

86. See, e.g., Shelby Mayes, "Campus Stance on Free Speech Facilitates Trauma Against Black Students," *Daily Californian*, September 22, 2017, www.dailycal.org/2017/09/22/campus-stance-free-speech -facilitates-trauma-black-students.

87. Claire Hansen, "New Title IX Guidance Gives Schools Choice in Sexual Misconduct Cases," *U.S. News & World Report*, September 26, 2017, www.usnews.com/news/education-news/articles/2017-09-26/new -title-ix-guidance-gives-schools-choice-in-sexual-misconduct-cases.

88. Don Gonyea, "Majority of White Americans Say They Believe Whites Face Discrimination," *NPR*, October 24, 2017, www.npr.org /2017/10/24/559604836/majority-of-white-americans-think-theyre -discriminated-against.

89. Rahuldeep Gill, "Memory as Benevolence: Toward a Sikh Ethics of Liberation," in *Memory and Hope: Forgiveness, Healing & Interfaith Relations*, ed. Alon Goshen-Gottstein, Maryland (Lexington Books, 2015), 89–106.

ABOUT THE EDITOR

Arjun Singh Sethi is a community activist, civil rights lawyer, writer, and professor based in Washington, DC. He
works closely with Muslim, Arab, South Asian, and Sikh
communities and advocates for racial justice, equity, and
social change at the local and national levels. His writing has appeared on CNN and in *The Guardian*, *Politico*
magazine, *USA Today*, *Los Angeles Times*, and the *Washington Post*, and he is featured regularly on national radio
and television. He holds faculty appointments at Georgetown University Law Center and Vanderbilt University
Law School and presently co-chairs the American Bar
Association's National Committee on Homeland Security,
Terrorism, and Treatment of Enemy Combatants.

PUBLISHING IN THE
PUBLIC INTEREST

Thank you for reading this book published by The New Press. The New Press is a nonprofit, public interest publisher. New Press books and authors play a crucial role in sparking conversations about the key political and social issues of our day.

We hope you enjoyed this book and that you will stay in touch with The New Press. Here are a few ways to stay up to date with our books, events, and the issues we cover:

- Sign up at www.thenewpress.com/subscribe to receive updates on New Press authors and issues and to be notified about local events
- Like us on Facebook: www.facebook.com/new pressbooks
- Follow us on Twitter: www.twitter.com/thenew press

Please consider buying New Press books for yourself; for friends and family; or to donate to schools, libraries, community centers, prison libraries, and other organizations involved with the issues our authors write about.

The New Press is a 501(c)(3) nonprofit organization. You can also support our work with a tax-deductible gift by visiting www.thenewpress.com/donate.